ELEMENTARY HARMONY
and
COUNTERPOINT

ERIC ROLLINSON

ISBN 0-88797-121-0

FREDERICK HARRIS MUSIC

529 Speers Rd., Oakville, Ontario, Canada
L6K 2G4

"My thanks are due to Dr. Ettore Mazzoleni, Principal of the Royal Conservatory of Music of Toronto, who read the original manuscript; and to Mr. F. R. C. Clarke, Mus. B., who read the proofs for me."

FOREWORD

Harmony and Counterpoint should be studied with a good teacher, not self-taught from a text-book. Few teachers, however, have sufficient time to write out all the facts in front of the student, and most teachers therefore make use of some kind of text-book to provide those facts. This book is intended to explain the facts, "rules", usages, idioms and special techniques *in the briefest possible way.* Undoubtedly, students will require further expansion of the facts from their teachers. No effort has been made to mention every possible "exception"—some of these seem to us a little confusing and dangerous to elementary students, and can better be added by the teacher at his discretion.

A sufficient number of exercises has been provided for purposes of "drill", but the object should be to advance the student to such a point where he can work on actual complete melodies and basses—plenty of material is provided in the examination papers of the various colleges and conservatories of music. Such complete melodies or basses require the student, not merely to use each tool properly but also to select the appropriate tool.

ERIC ROLLINSON.

CONTENTS

HARMONY AND PART WRITING FOR FOUR VOICES

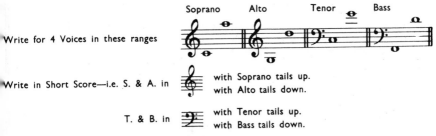

Write for 4 Voices in these ranges

Write in Short Score—i.e. S. & A. in
with Soprano tails up.
with Alto tails down.

T. & B. in
with Tenor tails up.
with Bass tails down.

Notice the difference between, say ... *and* ...

and you will realise why the direction of the tails is important.

We shall first study major scales only, the triads on I, IV, and V only, in root position only:—

These three are all major common chords.

Since there are three notes in each triad, and four voices to provide for, it is obvious that either Root, or 3rd, or 5th must be sung by two voices simultaneously at unison, or octave, or double-octave.

Rule: Double the root, or double the 5th: do not double 3rd of major common chord.

Rule: Never omit 3rd; 5th may be omitted *freely* —in which case triple the root.

Rule: S. & A., A. & T., may be as wide as an 8ve apart but not wider. T. & B. may be as wide apart as you like.

The following shows many different arrangements of Tonic triad of C, within the ranges above and within the rules about doubling and distribution:—

etc.

—and many more are possible.

Exercise: Write two dozen or more different arrangements of the triad of F (IV in C) and show them to your teacher.

F.H. 2894

The foregoing facts concerned *static* chords only. Now in order to move from one chord to another the following rules and pieces of special technique are necessary.

Make the parts move as *smoothly* as possible—do not worry about dullness in the parts at this stage: a note repeated several times in one voice is unavoidable and good—

Good

Rule: The Leading-Note should not be doubled, whatever the chord. [It will occur at present as 3rd of V only.]
The Leading-Note part normally proceeds to the Tonic [hence the name].

It may be transferred from one voice to another—then the *last* voice to sing it should move to Tonic:—

Later, you will need to know that the Leading-Note may move down the scale to Submediant if it is preceded by Tonic:—

etc.

No two voices should move in consecutive perfect 5ths or 8ves—consecutive 5ths have an awkward effect and may destroy the "tonality" [i.e., sense of what is the Tonic] and consecutive 8ves emphasise the particular voice-part, reducing the parts to three also. Ask your teacher.

Awful

IV V

This has consecutive 8ves between A. & B., and consecutive 5ths between T. & B.

Note well the word "move" above—you can repeat the *same* 8ve or the *same* 5th and there is nothing objectionable:—

etc., is good—the tenor and bass consecutive 8ves and 5ths have no *movement*.

SPECIAL TECHNIQUE for IV—V:—

See that *root* of IV is doubled [not 5th].
Make doubled root and 5th of IV BOTH
FALL.

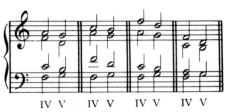

Progressions:— The movement of one chord to a *different* chord is called a progression.

Any chord used on a strong beat may be repeated (used again) on weak beat or between the beats.
For strong beat, *change* chord.

Progressions $\left\{\begin{array}{l} I—IV \\ I—V \end{array}\right.$ $\begin{array}{l} IV—I \\ IV—V \end{array}$ $\left.\begin{array}{l} V—I \\ \end{array}\right\}$ are all good progressions.

V—IV is awkward: use it rarely, and then only with this SPECIAL TECHNIQUE for V—IV.

V with its 5th in Sop., followed by

IV with its root doubled in Soprano.

Exercises: Write (1) I—IV—V in D major, B♭ major, F♯ major.
(2) IV—V—I in E♭ major, G major, D♭ major.
(3) V—IV—I in B♭ major, D major, F major.

(4) Add S.A.T. to the following Bass parts:—

Up to now we have said nothing about good leaps and bad leaps except for the general advice "write smooth parts". Now a more detailed list is necessary. The human voice works best moving by step. The following leaps are good and should be memorised:—

Minor 3rd; Major 3rd; Perfect 4th; Perfect 5th;
Minor 6th; Major 6th is less good—hard to sing in tune unless "covered" by 8ve or unison:—

8ve leap good only if the note *before* the 8ve leap and the note *after* it are both *within* the 8ve leap.

Good   Awful

Diminished 5th leap good between Subdominant and Leading-Note if followed by Tonic.

Good.

BAD LEAPS: all the others, viz. intervals wider than 8ve, 7th, all augmented interval leaps, and all diminished interval leaps.

Note the following

Bad

—compare with above.

CADENCES. The word means "falling", and refers to the way one's voice behaves in indicating punctuation in spoken language. Every phrase in classical music is brought to a close by a two-chord formula. The *last* of the two chords is normally accented. The cadence at the end of a piece must be Perfect or Plagal.

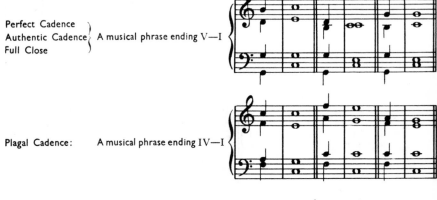

Perfect Cadence
Authentic Cadence } A musical phrase ending V—I
Full Close

Plagal Cadence: A musical phrase ending IV—I

Imperfect Cadence
Half Cadence } A musical phrase ending with V, approached by any good progression, at the moment IV—V or I—V.
Half Close

The Interrupted Cadence or False Close or Deceptive Cadence will be explained later.

Exercises: Add A.T.B. to the following Soprano. Choose cadence first; then choose chords, symbolizing as you go; then make a bass out of the roots of the chords; then add A. & T.

Cadence wanted

MINOR KEYS

Use the *harmonic* form of minor scale:

Remember that VII needs an accidental in front of it to raise it to be a semitone below Tonic, otherwise it is *not* a Leading-Note—most students remember this only 9 times out of 10.
The Leading-Note is very difficult to approach without a poor leap:—

—the only suitable note to approach Leading-Note from below is the Dominant

As a general guide: Approach Leading-Note *from Dominant only* from below, or from any note above.

Sometimes a piece in a minor key *ends* with a *major* common chord:—
This idiom [goodness knows why!] is called a Tièrce de Picardie

In the following exercises, an accidental ♯, ♭, ♮, under a bass note calls for the THIRD ABOVE that bass note to be ♯, ♭, ♮, accordingly.

The ending of the above piece would be figured:—

The inflection can go in any voice, of course.

Exercises on minor keys :—

(1) Write I—IV—V in C minor, G minor, F minor.
(2) Write IV—V—I in E minor, A minor, and [Tierce de Picardie] B minor.
(3) Write V—IV—I in G minor, B♭ minor, F♯ minor.
(4) Add S.A.T. to the following :

(5) Add A.T.B. to the following for Soprano:—

SUBMEDIANT TRIAD—VI

C major in a major key is a minor common chord—the 3rd of a minor common chord may occasionally be doubled, although root or 5th doubled is preferable.

C minor in a minor key is a major common chord.

Progressions:

I—VI	VI—II
II—VI	VI—IV } All good.
V—VI	VI—V

IV—VI   VI—I   — Not so good: explanation later.

V—VI and VI—V — great danger of "consecutives" and other serious faults!

SPECIAL TECHNIQUE for   V—VI and VI—V   Double 3rd of VI, and also Make 2 voices rise, 2 fall.

V—VI is the Interrupted Cadence, Deceptive Cadence or False Close if it occurs at the end of a phrase.
VI—V is an Imperfect Cadence if it occurs at the end of a phrase.
ⓧ Double the 3rd of VI even though here, in a minor key, it is a major 3rd—there is no way of avoiding more serious faults.

SUPERTONIC TRIAD—II

C major in a major key is a minor common chord.

C. minor in a minor key is a diminished triad—NOT TO BE USED until dim. triads have been studied.

Progressions:

I—II	VI—II
IV—II	II—V
V—II	II—VI

All good.

| II—IV | Not so good. |
| II—I | Ugly. |

SPECIAL TECHNIQUE for I—II: Adapt and use the special techniques for IV—V or for V—VI — whichever is convenient, to avoid consecutives.

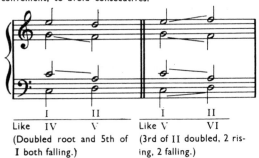

Like IV   V   Like V   VI
(Doubled root and 5th of   (3rd of II doubled, 2 ris-
I both falling.)   ing, 2 falling.)

Exercises:—(1) Write I—II—V—VI in E♭, A, F, B majors.
(2) Write I—II—VI—V in D, B♭, E majors.
(3) Add S.A.T. to the following for Bass:—

(a)   (b)

(c)   (d)

(4) Add A.T.B. to the following for Soprano. II and VI should be used as opportunities arise:—

(a) [G major]   (b) [F major]

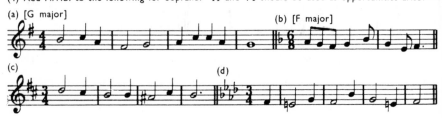

(c)   (d)

F.H. 2894

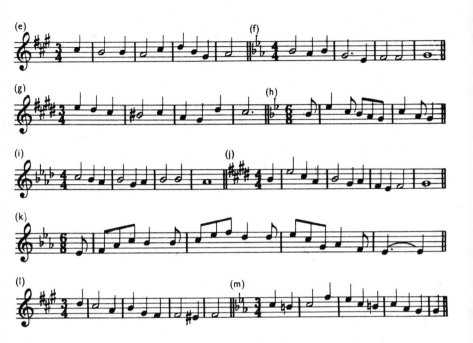

CHOICE OF CHORDS

We are shortly going to study the *inversions* of triads, but before that something further should be said about the nature of Progression. Up to now, the bass of a chord has been its root. After this, the bass may be the the root, or 3rd from root, or sometimes the 5th. *Progression depends on the way the ROOT behaves, NOT the bass.*

The root is thought of as always moving UP: this is for convenience— for if the root moves up a 4th it will reach the same note as if it had moved down a 5th; down a 3rd would be the same as·up a 6th:—

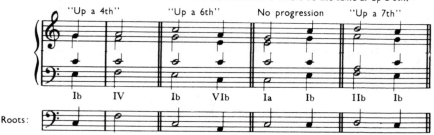

Ib IV   Ib VIb   Ia Ib   IIb Ib

Roots:

Examples of progressions: "Up a 2nd"—I—II, II—III, III—IV, IV—V, V—VI, VI—VII, VII—I are all the possible ones.

"Up a 4th"—I—IV, II—V, III—VI, IV—VII, V—I, VI—II, VII—III, are all the possible ones.

Consider the following passage, which is more a convenient diagram than music itself:—

The roots are:—

The roots move UP:— 4   6   5 ——— 7   7   5 ——— 4   3   7   4

(x) The root of Cadential Ic is V, not I—explanation later.

When the root moves UP a 2nd, 4th, 5th, or 6th—the progression is bound to be good, whatever the chords: though a few (involving III) may be objectionable on grounds of *counterpoint*, not harmony. Generally speaking, the above is true: and III will not be introduced for some time, hence the difficulty will not arise.

When the root moves UP a 7th—look at the chords! If they are VI—V, that is good.

Others—tolerable if second chord is in first inversion: II—Ia ugly;
II—Ib tolerable; V—IVa ugly usually; V—IVb much better.

When the root moves UP a 3rd—Never very good.

Tolerable when second chord is on weak beat, or between beats.
Bad when second chord is on strong beat.

Now this boils down to a very easy formula, like a telephone number: **2456/73.**

Most progressions will be with the root moving up a 2nd, 4th, 5th, 6th—where "Up a 7th" or "Up a 3rd" is convenient, see that the above advice about them is taken.

The tables of good progressions, not-so-good progressions, and bad progressions given earlier will be found to agree with the above, and may now be forgotten.

But do remember the rules for *repeated* chords [i.e., *no* progression] which are here given in different words:—

In approaching strong beat, change chord [i.e., make a progression].

In approaching weak beat, chord may be repeated [i.e., progression not necessary].

FIRST INVERSIONS

Root position   1st Inversion
IVa   IVa   IVb   IVb

When 3rd of chord is the bass note, chord is said to be in First Inversion.

Root position is indicated as Ia, Va, etc.   }
1st Inversion is indicated as Ib, Vb, etc.   } in symbols.

In Figured Bass, figure 6 [short for $\frac{6}{3}$] under a bass-note calls for first inversion:—

Counting up from the bass note, Root is a 6th above, }
                 5th from root is a 3rd above, } hence the figuring.

Doubling: Same principle as Root position—i.e., double root or 5th from root.
             Or, do not double bass of $\frac{6}{3}$, because this is 3rd from root.

Uses: (1) To make a smoother bass part.
             (2) In approaching an accent.
             (3) Certain progressions are tolerable if second chord is in first inversion.
             (4) VII is good as VIIb, also II of minor key as IIb.
             (5) To avoid certain "consecutives".

(1) To make a smoother bass.

     The following melody

     Might well be harmonized

I   I   IV   I   II   V   I

Which, using only root positions would give this result:—

which is good in its way, with a very firm bass.

Now, using the same chords, but judiciously fitting in a few of them in first inversion, we get this:—

which has a much smoother bass, more graceful.

Ib   Ib   Vb

F H. 2894

(2) A chord may be used again on strong beat [no progression] if its *bass*-note change—i.e., a change from root position to first inversion or vice versa.

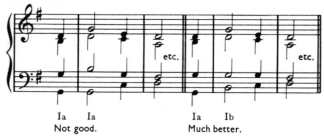

Ia   Ia   Ia   Ib
Not good.   Much better.

(3) Progressions "Up a 7th" are crude [except VI—V] if second chord is in root position, but tolerable if second chord is in first inversion.

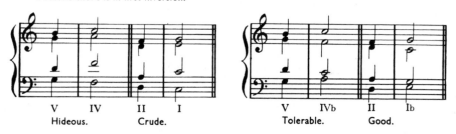

V   IV   II   I   V   IVb   II   Ib
Hideous.   Crude.   Tolerable.   Good.

(4) The Leading-Note triad [VII] may be used freely, as if it were a concord, in VIIb position.

It is **especially** common and useful between Ib and Ia, or between Ia and Ib.
Double 3rd from root of VII [i.e., bass of VIIb] if possible, or else 5th from root [i.e., 3rd from bass of VIIb].

Ib VIIb Ia   Ia VIIb Ib

[Do *not* double root of VII, because this is Leading-Note of the key.]

VIIb will deputise for V at any time—
for example VIIb—I   will do for a Perfect Cadence.
          VIIb—VI will do for an Interrupted Cadence.
  N.B.   VIIb—VI ["Up a 7th"] does not sound ugly because
          VIIb sounds so much like V.
But since VIIb sounds too much like V⁷, VIIb—V is weak.

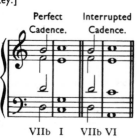

Perfect   Interrupted
Cadence.   Cadence.

VIIb I   VIIb VI

Similarly, II of minor key, which is a diminished triad, may be used freely as IIb. Double *any* note of IIb.

(5) The following fragment

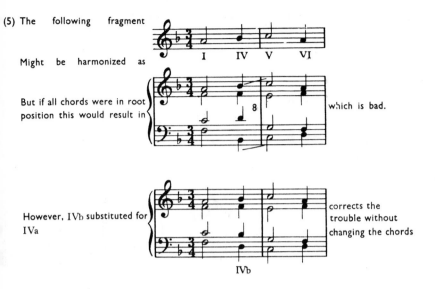

I   IV   V   VI

Might be harmonized as

But if all chords were in root position this would result in

which is bad.

However, IVb substituted for IVa

corrects the trouble without changing the chords

IVb

CONSECUTIVE FIFTHS

Exceptions.

Consecutive Perfect 5ths are, of course, crude.

A Perfect 5th may ALWAYS be followed by a diminished 5th. (a)

A diminished 5th may sometimes be followed by a Perfect 5th, but —

(b) the bass part must not be involved [5ths among S.A.T. only], and also

(c) the Perfect 5th must be the *higher* of the two.

(a)   Good.   Bad (b)   Good.   Bad (c)   All good.

—these exceptions are necessary in dealing with VIIb, and, later, V^7

EXTERIOR 8ve and Perfect 5th

Outside parts [S. & B. only] should not move by SIMILAR motion to 8ve or Perfect 5th.

—in vocal or string writing this will make the top part sound shrill.

The exceptions are important:—

Harmless when top part moves by STEP:—

Harmless between two positions of the same chord:
  [i.e., no change in harmony].

5th harmless when top part falls a 3rd between II and V or VI and II:—

8ve harmless when second chord is a Cadential $\frac{6}{4}$ or an Appoggiatura $\frac{6}{4}$:—

[This will be necessary later when $\frac{6}{4}$ chords are studied.]

compare with first example above.

Exercises:—

(1) Add A. & T.:—

(2) Add S.A.T.:—

I   Vb   I   IVb   IV   Ib   VIIb   I

I VIIb Ib IV VIIb Ib   IIb   V   I

(3) Add S.A.T.   Treat the following as Unfigured Basses, choosing the chords yourself.

[In choosing chords, a moment's thought will show that Mediant in the bass must be Ib always, since the alternative IIIa has not been studied.   Similarly, Leading-Note in bass must be Vb, since VIIa is ugly.]

16

(4) Add A.T.B.

First, choose cadences, and indicate by symbols.

Second, choose the approach-chord to each cadence.

Third, start at beginning of each phrase and choose chords, concentrating on good progressions [2, 4, 5, 6, / 7, 3] and symbolizing as you go.

Fourth—out of the chosen chords write a smooth bass-part, using root positions and first inversions to secure smoothness.   A moment's thought will show that if the 3rd of the chosen chord is in the Soprano the chord must be in root position, since a first inversion would cause 3rd to be doubled in Soprano and Bass.

Fifth, add A. & T.—but do NOT begin to do this until ALL chords are chosen and Bass-part is complete.

F.H. 2894

UNESSENTIAL NOTES

Chiefly Passing Notes, Auxiliaries, etc.

[Changing notes are left to be dealt with in 2-part Counterpoint, 3rd Species.]

General Function: To produce a *flowing* effect.

Class I—Those in common use by 1500. A.D.

PASSING NOTES.

—these join any two harmony-notes [or, "essential notes"] which happen to be a 3rd apart. On weak beats, or between the beats. In any voice.

—May be used (a) Singly.

              (b) Two together, in similar motion, a 3rd apart.

              (c) Two together, in similar motion, a 6th apart.

              (d) Two together, in contrary motion, an 8ve apart.

              (e) Two consecutively, joining the 5th of a chord with the root above it, or from root down to 5th.

Perhaps the following is clearer:

Passing Notes, Auxiliaries, etc., never correct an otherwise-faulty passage:

Bad   Equally
Bad

—but may cause trouble by introducing "consecutives" in an otherwise blameless passage:—

Good   Bad

18

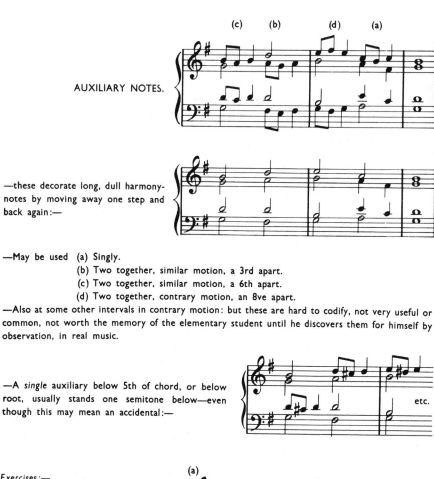

AUXILIARY NOTES.

(c) (b)   (d)   (a)

—these decorate long, dull harmony-
notes by moving away one step and
back again:—

—May be used (a) Singly.
   (b) Two together, similar motion, a 3rd apart.
   (c) Two together, similar motion, a 6th apart.
   (d) Two together, contrary motion, an 8ve apart.

—Also at some other intervals in contrary motion: but these are hard to codify, not very useful or common, not worth the memory of the elementary student until he discovers them for himself by observation, in real music.

—A *single* auxiliary below 5th of chord, or below
root, usually stands one semitone below—even
though this may mean an accidental:—

Exercises:—

(1) Decorate the following with passing-
    notes in any voices:—

F.H. 2894

(2) Decorate the following with auxiliary-notes in any voices:—

(a)

(b)

(c)

(3) Harmonize the following fragments by adding A.T.B. Notes encircled should be regarded as passing-notes or auxiliaries, *not* harmony-notes:—

(a)

(b)

(c)

(d)

THE MELODIC MINOR SCALE

Think of the minor scale as having alternative forms of
Submediant:— 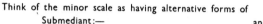 and Seventh Degree:—

C minor 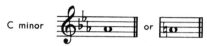 or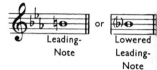

Leading-Note   Lowered Leading-Note

Both forms may be used—

AS HARMONY NOTES.

The raised Submediant:— 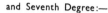 had best be preceded by Dominant or Tonic.

It must move to the Leading-Note which in turn usually moves to the Tonic.

It may be harmonized as factor of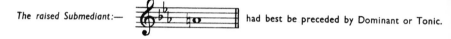

IV(♮3)   II(♮5)   ♮ VI

[Dim. triad—not in root position.]

Examples:

The lowered Leading-Note:  had best be preceded by Tonic or Dominant.

It must move to the ordinary Submediant which in turn usually moves to Dominant.

It may be harmonized as factor of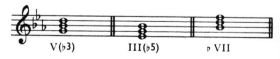

V(♭3)   III(♭5)   ♭ VII

The Dominant, when it arrives, had better be harmonized by V with the *ordinary* Leading-Note, otherwise the tonality may be uncertain. ["Tonality" is explained later.]

Examples:

(x) N.B. *Lowered* Leading-Note may be doubled.

AS UNESSENTIAL NOTES: unaccented or accented — to avoid augmented 2nd leaps in any voice part:—

For example:—

—and so on: the student will readily discover these for himself by observation as he writes.

Exercises:—

(1) Complete the following for S.A.T.B.:—[Symbolize all chords.]

(2) Decorate the following fragments with unessential-notes:—

[B minor]

F.H. 2894

SECOND INVERSIONS OF TRIADS

When 5th of the triad is the bass-note, chord is said to be in second inversion. Second inversion is indicated in symbols as, e.g., IVc, Ic, Vc etc.

The typical root position  is like a strong man firmly planted on both feet. (a)

The typical first inversion  is the same strong man—but now he is balanced on one leg. (b)

The typical second inversion 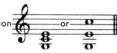 is still the same strong man—but now he is standing on his head. (c)

(a) Is strong enough for use anywhere.
(b) Is strong enough for use *almost* anywhere—but not at the end of a piece, and not usually so satisfactorily at cadences.
(c) Has a strong tendency to topple over into a root position chord on the same bass-note—play it and listen :—

—and therefore cannot be used freely, but only where this tendency to topple can be either *made use of* or *effectively concealed*.

There are five special ways of using it:—

        (1) Cadential $\frac{6}{4}$

        (2) Appoggiatura $\frac{6}{4}$ } these make use of the tendency to topple.

        (3) Auxiliary $\frac{6}{4}$

        (4) Passing $\frac{6}{4}$

        (5) Arpeggio $\frac{6}{4}$ } these conceal the tendency.

In Figured Bass, figures $\frac{6}{4}$ under a bass-note calls for second inversion:—

Counting up from bass-note, root is a 4th above, 3rd from root is a 6th above—hence the figuring. Double bass of $\frac{6}{4}$ preferably—this is not too important.

(1) _Cadential_ $\frac{6}{4}$:   Ic always.

                Strong beat always.

                Followed by Va always.

                Any chords which will lead to Va

                will lead through Ic to Va.

IV   Ic   V   IIb   VI

Where Cadential Ic is appropriate: at a cadence involving dominant triad, $\begin{cases} \text{V—I} & \text{(Perfect)} \\ \text{V—VI} & \text{(Interrupted)} \\ \text{?—V} & \text{(Imperfect)} \end{cases}$

where the note immediately before V chord is Tonic, Mediant, or Dominant of the key, <u>USE Ic for it.</u>

For example, let the note before this cadence :—  be G, B, or D, then the best choice of

chord is Ic

Notes: (a)   It is not important that 6th from bass of Ic fall to 5th and 4th fall to 3rd, though this has often been asserted: that movement is, of course, the natural tendency of those notes, but if you confine your uses of Cadential Ic to occasions when that tendency can be gratified you will use the chord _seldom_.

          (b)   Occasionally and very rarely Va in the cadence will come on strong beat—then if Cadential Ic were used it would occur on weak beat, which would be ugly; this exception rarely occurs:

24

(c) Cadential Ic is tolerable on *second* beat of triple time:—

(d) Later, when you have studied the Dominant Seventh chord— Instead of Va, V⁷d may be used after Cadential Ic, but *not* any *other* inversion of V or V⁷. Since:—

is obviously good,

therefore—

is good also.

(2) *Appoggiatura* 6/4: IVc always.
Strong beat always.
Followed by Ia always.
Any chords which will lead to Ia will lead *through* IVc to Ia

—rather like a Cadential 6/4; often confused with it, even by professional theorists.

Remember—Cadential 6/4 is Ic,

Appoggiatura 6/4 is IVc. } always.

F.H. 2894

3) *Auxiliary* $\frac{6}{4}$.

It would be fascinating to speculate on how chance or the ingenuity of some unknown composer developed out of two simultaneous auxiliary-notes happening to produce a $\frac{6}{4}$:—

these typical idioms:—

I   IVc —   I   IVc   Ic   IIc

—Can be *any* triad in second inversion.

—Weak beat usually, or between beats—nauseating on strong beat.

—The chord *before* $\frac{6}{4}$, and also the one *after* $\frac{6}{4}$, must be a root position on the *same*

bass as the $\frac{6}{4}$.   N.B. that the 6th and 4th from bass need _not_ be auxiliary-notes.

—**Sometimes** called "Pedal $\frac{6}{4}$"—for reasons which will appear.

(4) *Passing* $\frac{6}{4}$.

Usually Vc between Ia and Ib or between Ib and Ia ⎫ Weak beat usually.
Or, Ic between IVa and IVb or between IVb and IVa ⎭

Double the bass of $\frac{6}{4}$ IN THE SOPRANO, and make S. & B. sing *the same three notes in* contrary motion.

For example:

Ib—Vc—Ia will produce "Three Blind Mice" in the bass

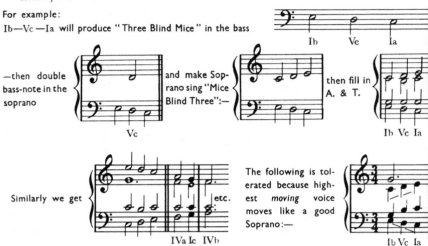

—then double bass-note in the soprano   and make Soprano sing "Mice Blind Three":—   then fill in A. & T.

Similarly we get   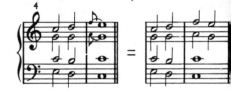   The following is tolerated because highest *moving* voice moves like a good Soprano:—

N.B.—The only case [in 4-part writing] where two 6 chords can beautifully follow one another—
                                                                                        4
Passing $\frac{6}{4}$ followed by Appoggiatura $\frac{6}{4}$.

The Soprano always sings Tonic, Supertonic, Subdominant, Mediant—that is, in major keys, Doh-Ray-Fah-Me.

(5) *Arpeggio* $\frac{6}{4}$.

—Any chord in second inversion.
—Must be preceded by same triad in root position or first inversion.
—*After* the $\frac{6}{4}$—there may be same triad yet again, and bass will move from $\frac{6}{4}$ by *leap*.

—Or there may be a *new* chord: which must be such that bass can move from $\frac{6}{4}$ by *step*.

Exercises:

(1) Write IV—Ic—Va—I in Eb, G minor, B.
(2) Write VI—Ic—V in D minor, F♯ minor, Bb.
(3) Write II —Ic—V—VI in F, A, E.

(4) Add S.A.T.:—
Mark the *name* of every 6 as you use it—"C", "P", "Aux.", "Arp.", "App.".

(6) Add A.T.B.:—

IVc   Ic   Ic   Ic Va   Ia Ic IVb   Ic Va VI   IVa Ib Vc   IVc I
Aux.   Cad.   Passing   Cad.   Arp.   Cad.   Pass. Appogg.

(7) [E min.]

IVc Ia   Ic   Ia   Ia   IVc_ I   VI   Ic   Va I
Aux.   Pass.   Cad.   Aux.   Cad.

28

(6) Add A.T.B., making whatever use of $\frac{6}{4}$ chords you can find:—

DOMINANT SEVENTH CHORD—V^7

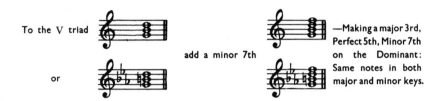

To the V triad   add a minor 7th   —Making a major 3rd, Perfect 5th, Minor 7th on the Dominant: Same notes in both major and minor keys.

or

V^7 is a discord: which means, not an ugly noise as most people suppose, but an *incomplete* chord—something which must be quitted in a certain special way, and sometimes approached in a special manner.

V^7 needs no special approach—any chord which will go before V triad will go before V^7.

V^7 must be followed by I ("Up a 4th") or VI ("Up a 2nd").

The 7th from root of $V^{7'}$ must fall a step.

The 3rd from root of V^7 must rise a step.

[V^7—VI: both root position—double 3rd of VI, and make 2 voices rise, 2 fall.]

<u>All</u> the inversions of V^7 are equally good—no need to avoid V^7c.

V^7b   Ia V^7c   Ia V^7c   VI V^7d   Ib

N.B.—V^7d ALWAYS resolves on Ib—nothing else will satisfy.

Notice especially the one-and-only case where 7th-note from root of V^7 may RISE instead of falling as usual:— V^7c — Ib

V^7c   Ib V^7c   Ib

F.H. 2894

Occasionally, V^7 may resolve on IV *inverted*—

Hideous.

N.B.—Never IV in root position:—the progression is "Up a 7th" and would be crude if IV were in root position.
3rd of V^7 rises as usual, but 7th from root STANDS FIRM.

V^7_a IVb V^7_b IVc I V^7_c IVc I V^7_d IVa
              (1)   (1)   (2)

(1) IVc is a good Appoggiatura $\frac{6}{4}$—but must occur on strong beat.

(2) Notice that V^7_d never can resolve in this way.

7th-note of V^7 [and 3rd, of course] may be transferred from one voice to another—resolving in the *last* voice to sing it:—

While the V^7 chord is sustained or repeated, 7th note may step or leap to any other factor of the chord, provided it gets back to the proper note of resolution at the change of harmony:—

In Figured Bass:—

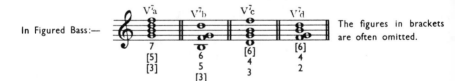

The figures in brackets are often omitted.

Notes which are *alphabetically* adjacent—like root and 7th—should not move to unison or octave:—

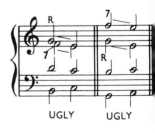

UGLY   UGLY

31

Exercises:

(1) Write V^7—I for S.A.T.B., and all the inversions with resolutions, in A major, F minor.

(2) Write IV—V^7_a—VI; VIb—V^7_b—I; IIb—V^7_c—Ia; IV—V^7_d—Ib in D minor.

(3) Write Ib—V^7_a—IVb—V^7_b—I

VIb—V^7_b—IVc (Appogg. $\frac{6}{4}$)—Ia $\Big\}$ in A♭, E.

IV—V^7_c—IVc —Ia

(4) Write V^7_c—Ib in D, B minor, F♯, B♭ minor.

(5) Complete the following by adding A. & T.:—

(6) Add S.A.T.:—

(7) Add A.T.B.:—

F.H. 2894

UNESSENTIAL NOTES

Class II—those not in general use until after 1600. A.D.

ACCENTED PASSING NOTES
and ACCENTED AUXILIARIES

—same as ordinary passing notes and auxiliaries, except for the accent.

—same principles for two simultaneously.

—somewhat more effective in descending to resolve.

—more *exciting* than ordinary ones—hence, preferable.

Most of the above passage could be treated with the earlier technique; but the effect is less *stirring* :—

Any unessential note, accented as well as unaccented, may be approached by LEAP; but it is always *quitted* by step—and if it resolve *upwards* into harmony-note it usually stands a *semitone* below its note-of-resolution—this may require an accidental.

Many very-chromatic sections of melody may be dealt with very simply using this technique: as an extreme example, who would imagine that this:—

could be harmonized with 3 chords ?

Single Changing Notes: where there are two harmony notes, the second a step below the first, the first may move *up* a step, then down a 3rd, thus:—

may be elaborated into

or such a figure as

may best be treated as

Notes of Anticipation: especially at cadences, a part may anticipate a note [or notes, in two parts] of the approaching chord:—

Exercises:

(1) Add A.T.B., using the suggested chords:—

(a)

I Ib   IV Ib   II IIb   V   V⁷d Ib Ia   VI II   Ic V⁷   I

(b)

I   I   IVb   V   V V⁷VI   IV IVb IIb   Ic   V V⁷d Ib   Ia   Ia

IVb IVa IVb   Ic   Ic   V⁷   VI   IV   Î(♮3)

(c)

I   Ib   IV   Ic   V⁷d Ib   Ia   IVb IIb   Ic V   V⁷   I   Ib   IV

V   V⁷   VI   IIb IIb   V   IVb V⁷   I

F.H. 2894

34

(2) Add A.T.B.:—

(a)

(b)

(c)

(d)

FIGURED BASS

The underlying principle is, that over every given bass note a 3rd and a 5th will be written, unless the 3rd is contradicted by figure 2 or 4, or the 5th contradicted by figure 6.

A root position triad therefore does not require figures $\frac{5}{3}$, which are taken for granted, and only written when $\frac{6}{4}$ is followed by $\frac{5}{3}$.

6 is short for $\frac{6}{3}$ and calls for the first inversion of a triad.

Since a $\frac{6}{4}$ is the trickiest of all chords to use, it is always *figured in full*—there is no abbreviation of $\frac{6}{4}$.

♯, ♭, ♮ alone under a bass-note calls for THIRD above bass-note to be figured accordingly. ♮5, ♯6, $\frac{♯4}{2}$ etc. are surely self-explanatory.

7, short for $\frac{7}{\frac{5}{3}}$ calls for a chord-of-the-seventh in root position.

$\frac{6}{5}$, short for $\frac{\frac{6}{5}}{3}$ calls for a chord-of-the-seventh in 1st inversion.

$\frac{4}{3}$, short for $\frac{\frac{6}{4}}{3}$ calls for a chord-of-the-seventh in 2nd inversion.

$\frac{4}{2}$, short for $\frac{\frac{6}{4}}{2}$ calls for a chord-of-the-seventh in 3rd inversion.

Line of continuation:—

calls for the chord above the note at the beginning of the line to be sustained or repeated until the end of the line:—

Bass-notes A, C, E are passing-notes.

Important unnessential notes are often included in the figuring—no complete catalogue of possibilities can be given but the following are typical :—

 calls for two 6ths above E, one a half-note long and one quarter-note C moving to B which is obviously a passing-note between C and A:

 calls for a V triad on 1st 2 beats, then 7 on 3rd beat

3 4 5＿‥‥calls for quarter-notes B, C, then half-note D.
5 4 3＿‥‥calls for quarter-notes D, C, then half-note B.
8＿＿＿7‥‥calls for dotted half-note G, then quarter-note F.

The "direct" like a small W on a line or space, is used to indicate pitch without indicating any particular time-value.

The following occurs frequently:

—Calling for the chords at the beginning of each line [I and V] to be held or repeated, with some voice moving in thirds above the bass.

MEDIANT TRIAD—III.—IN MAJOR KEY

[The two forms of III of minor key are dealt with elsewhere.]

According to traditional "rules", III must not be preceded or followed
by any chord containing the Subdominant of the scale, except in the middle
of a sequence.
II, IV, VII are therefore said to be unpleasant before or after III, though
this writer finds VII—III perfectly acceptable:—

VIIb III VI

If one voice is descending the scale from Tonic through Leading-Note to Submediant, III may be
followed by IV very effectively:

III   IV   IIIb IV

IIIb may be used without any restrictions in the middle of a chain of $\frac{6}{3}$ chords:—

IIIb   IIIb

Probably the real reasons why IIIa and IIIb are used so seldom are:—
  (1) In places where III would fit, some *other* chord would fit even better.
  (2) As shown later, IIIb sounds most frequently like a form of the Dominant Thirteenth
       chord in root position: and since *sound* is what matters, not appearance on paper, it
       will be discussed later in connection with V^{13}

Exercises:
  (1) Write (a) VI—III—Ib—IV—V in G, B♭ majors.
       (b) I-III—VI—V⁷b—I in F, A majors [see that III is not on strong beat.]

(2) Complete the following for S.A.T.B.:—

III   6   6 6 6
                                                                   5

F.H. 2894

38

TWO-PART WRITING

To add a bass [only] to a given melody.

The object is to make a piece which sounds complete in the two parts—not merely a top and a bottom part satisfactory when A. & T. are afterwards added. For perfect examples, see many of the little pieces in the "Anna Magdalena Notebook" of J. S. Bach.

Method: (1) Sing the given melody several times, thus determining the phrasing, which mark.

(2) Every Phrase must end with a cadence: indicate these by symbols as you choose them.

(3) Choose and indicate a good approach-chord to each cadence.

(4) Starting at the beginning of each phrase, write a bass part:—

The intervals between S. & B. on the main beats will generally be concords, preferably imperfect ones [3rds and 6ths] rather than perfect [5ths and 8ves].

8ve or P. 5th good as first or last chord of a phrase.

Many of the S. notes may be regarded as passing-notes or auxiliaries, accented or unaccented; unessential notes may also be used freely in the bass.

4th between S. & B. should generally imply some good use of 6.
4

7th between S. & B. should generally imply V^7—Dim. 5th and Aug. 4th are also good if they imply inversions of V^7.

Use a good proportion of Contrary motion.

Where Sop. moves slowly in long notes, make B. move quickly in short notes, and vice versa.

Example:—

—If this technique is followed, good progressions will nearly always result—no need to choose every chord: but be sure to choose very carefully the chords for the cadences.

F.H. 2894

COUNTERPOINT IN TWO PARTS

The word is short for "Pointcounterpoint"—"point" is an old word for "note", and the word means the art of writing notes against (counter to) other notes.
There are two distinct kinds of counterpoint:
"Free" counterpoint means the more-or-less instrumental style which began to grow from about A.D. 1600, culminating in the technique of J. S. Bach, and making use of any harmonic scheme right down to Brahms— seventh chords, 6 chords, modulation and chromaticism are all good.
_4

"Strict" counterpoint is quite different: it refers to the purely vocal style of the 16th century, as exemplified by Palestrina, but including the main technique of Lassus in the Netherlands and South Germany, Victoria in Spain, Byrde and his many great contemporaries in England. Here are the first principles and the

FIRST SPECIES.

A short tune in whole notes is provided, called a Cantus Firmus (Latin) or Canto Fermo (Italian) or C.F. for short. The art is to write a good tune above or below it, as requested—first of all a single note in Cpt. against each note in the C.F.
For students' purposes, C.F. is always made to end Supertonic—Tonic.
Cpt. must always end Leading-Note—Tonic.
First note of Cpt., if *above* C.F., must be P. 5th or 8ve above (or double 8ve).
First note of Cpt., if *below* C.F., must be Unison, 8ve, or double 8ve below.
Middle bars: Cpt. must be major or minor 3rd, major or minor 6th, P. 5th or 8ve above or below each note of C.F. N.B.—No discords, no P. 4th—which latter is a discord (men had long since discovered) when it occurs between the *bass* and any other voice.   No dim. or aug. intervals, which are discords.

—Have not more than 3 parallel thirds or sixths, which would be dull.

Leaps: Same as given in "Harmony"—which see.
—More will be said about First Species later; but get to work on acquiring some facility in writing good smooth tunes immediately, without bothering about the False Relation of the Tritone and other mysteries. Consecutive and Exterior 5ths and 8ves are bad.

40

SECOND SPECIES.

—Half-notes in Cpt., starting with half-note rest.

Beginning—
Ending— } same rules as First Species, which see.
First note of each middle bar—

The *second* note of each middle bar may be (a) a concord: which may be approached and quitted freely, by step or leap. P. 5th or 8ve or unison on 2nd beat are not objectionable.
(b) a passing note.
(c) an auxiliary note.

The chief difficulty in Second Species is to avoid a leap between 1st and 2nd note of each bar: try to get first notes of consecutive bars a 3rd apart (then passing-note will fit between them), or the same note (when auxiliary note will fit between). When Second Species is in the bass, leaps are often unavoidable in last three bars.

THIRD SPECIES.—Quarter-notes, starting with quarter-note rest.

Beginning—
Ending—   } same rules as First Species, which see.
First note of each middle bar—

EITHER 3rd OR 4th note of each middle bar [or both, of course] must be CONCORD.

The remaining quarter-notes [2nd, and 3rd or 4th] may be concords also—approached and quitted freely by step or leap; or they may be auxiliary notes or passing notes.

Changing-notes may be used sparingly; there are two kinds:—

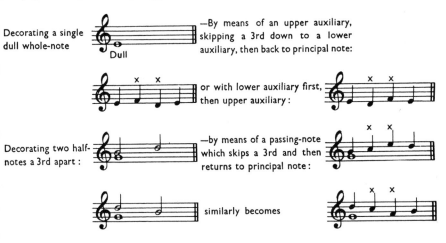

Decorating a single dull whole-note —By means of an upper auxiliary, skipping a 3rd down to a lower auxiliary, then back to principal note:

or with lower auxiliary first, then upper auxiliary :

Decorating two half-notes a 3rd apart : —by means of a passing-note which skips a 3rd and then returns to principal note :

similarly becomes

N.B.—In both kinds of changing-notes, 1st and 4th quarters are concords; 2nd and 3rd are, or may be, discords.

FOURTH SPECIES—Half-notes, the second of each bar tied to the first of the next bar.
Starts with half-note rest.

Beginning } same rules as First Species, q.v.
Ending

The SECOND note of each middle bar must be a CONCORD.

The first note of each middle bar may be—a concord: which may move freely by step or leap to
 another concord.

—a discord: which must step DOWN to a concord.

Occasionally a discord steps down and
still does not reach a concord:—

This will not do; some other
solution must be found.

FIFTH SPECIES.

—All the Species mingled: preferably mingled _within_ each bar [bar 5 above sounds well in the context,
but is not a good model of "mingling"; also, do not have more than 6 consecutive quarters, or 7 at
opening only. Each Species is governed by its own "rules".

PLUS—eighth-notes, in couples, on 2nd or 4th quarters of the bar only, approached and quitted
by step, used sparingly—not in consecutive bars.

Treatment of 4th Species when used as part of 5th Species:—

The note to be tied over must be a half-
note always:—

The note which _has_ been tied over, on first beat can be

—a concord, which may, if desired, be a quarter-note, and move freely
from 2nd quarter of the bar:—

—a discord: which must reach its proper note-of-resolution on the
THIRD quarter—NOT SECOND.

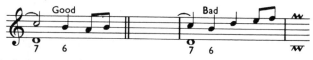

On 2nd quarter there may be an ornamental resolution—see below.

A half-note, on second half of the bar, preceded by shorter notes, should be tied over:—

F.H. 2894

—except in last-but-one bar; where the hesi-
tating effect is appropriate:

The following rhythm is not found in the 16th century:—

ORNAMENTAL RESOLUTION.

Before resolving on 3rd quarter, a 4th Species discord may, on 2nd quarter—

(a) Move down a 3rd, then up a 2nd to proper note-of-resolution.
(b) Move up a 2nd, then down a 3rd to proper note-of-resolution.
(c) Leap down to another note of the chord-of-resolution, then back up to the proper note-of-resolution.
(d) Join the leaps-of-a-third in (a) and (b) with an eighth-note passing note.

Ordinary procedure,
without ornament.

(a) developed by passing-note   (b) with passing-note
    added, joining D to B.   added, joining E to C.

44

CONSECUTIVES in Strict Counterpoint

Direct consecutive 5ths or 8ves are, of course, bad.

Second and Third Species:

Consecutives between adjacent first beats are bad always:—

—These should cause no trouble since you are advised to avoid 8ve and P. 5th on first beats of middle bars.

—Consecutives between adjacent *second* beats are bad only if *both* notes are "inside" or both "outside" notes:—

Consecutive 5ths good between adjacent second beats if at least one of the two is a passing-note or auxiliary :—

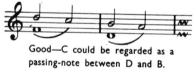   

An *intervening* change of harmony is sufficient to cover up "consecutives", even between adjacent *first*. beats:—

—both of these are good, though not advisable in two-part work owing to the thin effect of octave on 1st beat.

F.H. 2894

Consecutives in Fourth Species: everything is backwards, like "Alice through the Looking-Glass!"
Consecutives between second beats are usually bad:—

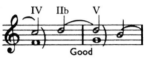

sounds like a decorated version of:

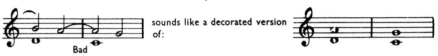

—between adjacent first beats usually harmless:—

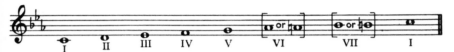

—the D in Soprano effectively changes the chord from IV to IIb which intervenes before V.

MINOR KEYS

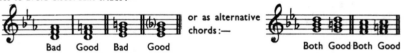

Think of scale as having two alternative 6th and 7th degrees, either of which may be used as harmony notes to avoid discordant triads :—

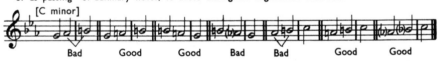

—or as passing—or auxiliary notes, to avoid unsingable augmented intervals:—

Be sure to establish minor key as early as possible by implying progressions V—I, V—VI, VIIb—I, as close to the beginning as possible. After that, what we should call "modulation to the relative major" is good: this is the only modulation allowed in Strict Cpt., and would have been explained by the 16th century writers as something quite different:—

F.H. 2894

STRICT COUNTERPOINT IN THREE PARTS

—C.F. moves in whole notes.
—One other voice moves in First Species—i.e., whole-notes.
—One other voice moves in 2nd, 3rd, 4th, or 5th Species.

Beginning: If the First Species part enters *above* the C.F., it may start on 3rd above C.F., if desired—but not 3rd or 6th *below* C.F.

Middle bars: When concord is required (as on 1st beat except in 4th Species, for example) ALL THREE VOICES must be in concord.

$\frac{5}{3}$ and $\frac{6}{3}$ positions of major and minor common chords are concords to be used freely. Dim. triads (VII of major keys, II and VII of minor keys) may be used freely *in first inversion—as if they were concords*: but root position of each is a discord. 4th between *bass* and any other part is a discord: hence $\frac{6}{4}$ is discord.

When possible, try to get *complete* triad on first beat (root, 3rd, 5th) but do not sacrifice the interest of the melodies for this purpose: two roots and a third are quite good, one root and two thirds tolerable; even two fifths and one third may sound well in certain contexts.

N.B.—The following:—

—*either* 3rd *or* 4th quarter must be concord with *both* the other voices simultaneously; but C is a discord with bass-note G, though concord with Soprano E, and D is discord with Soprano E, though a concord with Bass-note G. There are many similar cases.

An occasional repeated note is tolerable in the First Species part only.

The Ending: C.F. (which may be top, middle, or bass part) ends Supertonic—Tonic.
One other voice [either the First Species or the other] must end Leading-Note—Tonic.
The remaining part may end on Mediant, if desired, except in the *bass*.
The remaining part completes penultimate chord as Va, Vb, or VIIb—whichever is convenient: no other chord is possible here.

Examples of endings:—

STYLE in Strict Counterpoint

—interest is secured in 2nd, 3rd, 5th Species by development, sequence and imitation within the counterpoint itself: several examples of this are apparent in the examples given.

—When all or both parts are in First Species, the best way to lend interest is by means of imitative entries:— Have Cpt. enter at 2nd, 3rd, 4th bar, preceded by rests.

Make Cpt. enter imitating the first 2. 3, or 4 bars of C.F.

The imitation need NOT be exact.

For this purpose, 1st note of Cpt. may be at _any_ concordant interval above or below C.F.

There are _always_ several possible ways of doing this: the ideal is to work several solutions:—

(a)

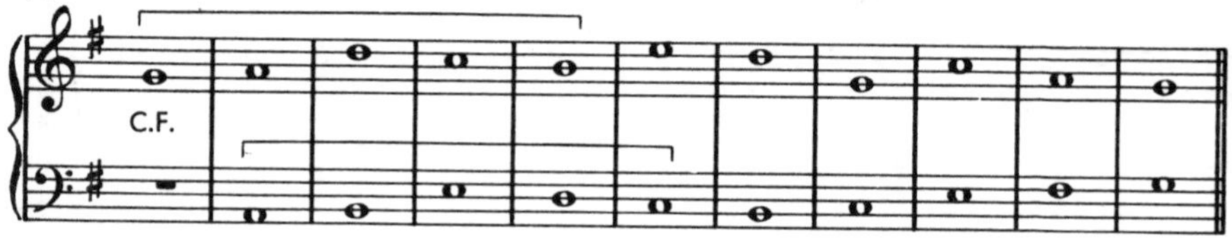

C.F.

(b)

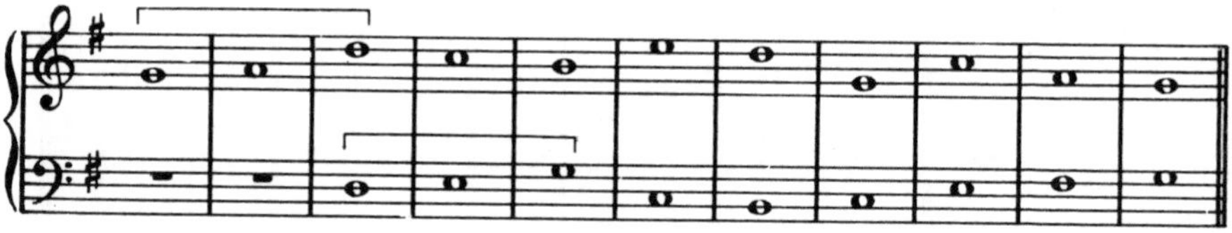

(c)

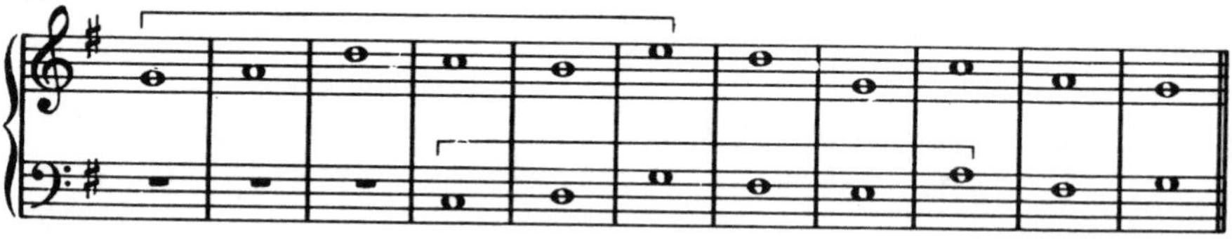

—and choose the best: (a) or (c), probably (a), is best here.

ALWAYS use this technique.

Three parts in First Species: use same technique:—

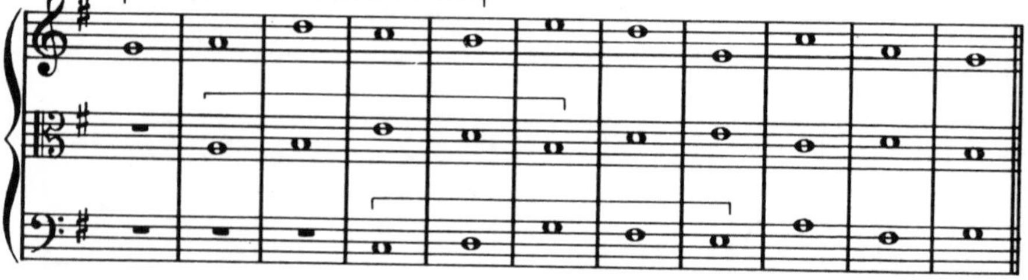

—in three voices, last entry could be as late as bar 9 in a _long_ exercise—in a shorter one, overlap them as shown above.

The TRITONE: the augmented 4th between Subdominant and Leading-Note of a major or minor scale—six semitones = 3 tones, hence the name.

In 16th century the "False Relation of the Tritone" was found objectionable if both the parts concerned moved by STEP:—

If you notice it, it is easy to avoid—merely by making one [either] of the voices LEAP:—

 —the Tritone is present, but harmless.

Great care must be taken, especially in two parts, with a moving part in the bass, to avoid an implied $\frac{6}{4}$. It is true that a note continues to sing in our memories after it has ceased until it is effectively contradicted—C by appearance of B, etc.

Hence this:— [music] will sound like [music] which give a $\frac{6}{4}$ effect on second beat.

Similarly, [music] is wrong, but [music] is good

IVa   IIa   Vb

[music] is good: it sounds as [music]

VIb   IVa

ROOT POSITION OF AUGMENTED AND DIMINISHED TRIADS

These are VIIa in major and minor keys  —which are diminished triads.

IIa in minor keys —another diminished triad.

and IIIa of minor keys —which is an augmented triad.

Special Technique: The 5th from root of each triad should be "*prepared*"—that is, sung just previously by the *same* voice as a *concord:*—[N.B.—Memorize this term—it will be important later.]

VIIa   VIIa   VIIa   IIa   IIIa

Double 3rd of VII if possible, root of II or III if possible.
(1) IVb here used with 3rd from root raised, to avoid augmented 2nd in bass.
In resolving, diminished 5th should FALL a step,
        or augmented 5th should RISE a step.
Any chord which ordinarily makes a good progression after VII, II, or III may be used, provided it contains the proper note of resolution:—

VIIa IIIb   VIIa Ia   VIIa Ia   IIa Va   IIIa VI

Exercises:—

(1) Write (a) Ia—IIa—VIIa—I in G, B♭.
Write (b) Ia—IVb—VIIa—I in D min., F♯ min., B♭ min.
   [Use IVb with raised 3rd, i.e. bass-note—to avoid aug. 2nd interval in bass.]
Write (c) Ia—Va—IIIa—VIa—VIb—IIa—V⁷b—I in G min., B min., F min.

(2) Add A. & T.:—

(3) Add S.A.T.:—

F.H. 2894

SECONDARY [or Diatonic] SEVENTH CHORDS

In studying harmony, we began with a major scale

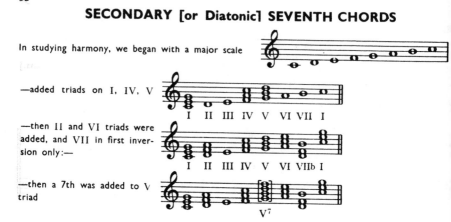

—added triads on I, IV, V

I II III IV V VI VII I

—then II and VI triads were added, and VII in first inversion only:—

I II III IV V VI VIIb I

—then a 7th was added to V triad

V⁷

—and finally a few facts about III triad were given:—

and some directions for using VII in root position

III   VIIb

The next study is by adding a diatonic 7th to each of the triads:—

I⁷   II⁷ III⁷ IV⁷   V⁷ VI⁷ VII⁷

None of these secondary sevenths has exactly the same quality as a dominant seventh chord, which has a major 3rd, perfect 5th, minor 7th.

I⁷   IV⁷   II⁷ III⁷ VI⁷   VII⁷

have major 7th notes.   have minor 3rds.   is different from all the others—it has a minor 3rd, dim. 5th and minor 7th.

Nevertheless, one set of "rules" will be sufficient for the three new kinds of seventh chord. Before coming to the rules, let us point out that *all* the inversions of each are good, and that the figuring is the same principle as in V⁷:—

7, short for $\frac{7}{5}$ means the root position of *any* seventh-chord.

5. short for $\frac{6}{3}$ means the first inversion of *any* seventh-chord—and so on.

III⁷ and VII⁷ can be used *freely*, even though III and VII triads require special treatment. The 7th note from the root should, *if possible*, be "prepared":—

V   I⁷   Vb   I⁷d   Vb   I⁷a

Poor

By adding a 7th note to a triad we do not change the root progression—V—I is good, hence V—I⁷ is good also; IV—I is good, hence IV—I⁷ is good also—even though IV before I⁷ makes it impossible to prepare 7th note of the latter: no need to refuse the progression; merely approach 7th note by step:—

Good.

In resolving, 7th note normally FALLS a STEP. [Like 7th of V⁷.]
In resolving, 3rd note is quite free to step or leap up or down. [Unlike V⁷.]
The chord of resolution is on a root a 4th or 2nd higher than root of seventh-chord.
That is:— I⁷   resolves on IV   or II   [generally IV]
            II⁷   resolves on V   or III   [generally V]
            III⁷ resolves on VI   or IV   [generally VI]
            IV⁷   resolves on VII or V   [generally V]
            [V⁷   resolves on I   or VI—same pattern of root progression, you see.]
            VI⁷   resolves on II   or VII [generally II]
            VII⁷ resolves on III or I   [generally I]

Specimens:—

I⁷b IVa   II⁷c Va   III⁷a VIa   IV⁷c Vb   VI⁷d IIb   VII⁷b Ib

A $\frac{6}{4}$ chord, in style of Cadential $\frac{6}{4}$ [i.e., strong beat, followed by chord of resolution in _root_ position etc.] may occur between the seventh-chord and its chord of resolution. Especially II⁷ often resolves in this way, with the true Cadential $\frac{6}{4}$ of the key occurring between it and Va:—

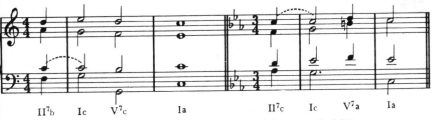

II⁷b   Ic   V⁷c   Ia   II⁷c   Ic   V⁷a   Ia

N.B.—In that case, 7th note of the seventh-chord will _stand firm_ instead of falling.

54

One seventh-chord may resolve on another seventh-chord; indeed there may be a whole chain of seventh-chords—one resolving on another properly and breaking off at any convenient point—$II^7 - V^7 - I^7 - IV^7 - VII^7$ etc. as follows:

II⁷a V⁷c   I⁷a IV⁷c Vb   I

Ornamental Resolutions: exactly the same style as V^7, which see.
The 5th from the root can, of course, be omitted from any seventh-chord—double the root in that case.

Exercises:—

[Symbolize all chords: these, and your own.

(1) Write chords before and after the following
    secondary seventh chords:—
    [Some may be in the major key, some in the
    minor, and some may work in both.]

(2) Add S.A.T.:—[Symbolize all chords.]
(a)
(b)
(c)
(d)

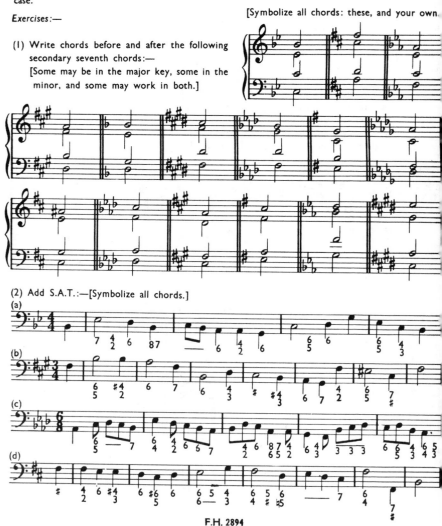

F.H. 2894

3) Write for S.A.T.B.:—
  (a) IVa—II^{7}a—Ic—V^{7}a—Ia in C minor, F, A♭.
  (b) VIa—IV^{7}a—Ic—Va—Ia in F♯ minor, G minor, E♭.

4) Add A.T.B.:—

(5) Add S.A.T.:—
(a) [Symbolize all chords.]

(6) Add A.T.B.:—

F.H. 2894

56

SEVENTH CHORDS—Exceptional Resolutions.

Any seventh chord *may* resolve with its root "rising a 7th" if the second chord is inverted. The seventh-note may stand firm or fall a second, whichever is convenient.

Examples:

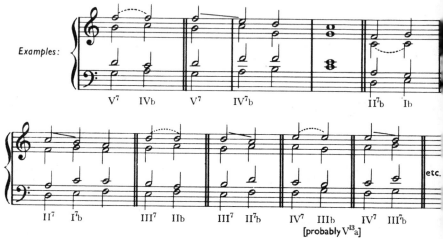

V⁷ IVb   V⁷ IV⁷b   II⁷b Ib

II⁷ I⁷b   III⁷ IIb   III⁷ II⁷b   IV⁷ IIIb   IV⁷ III⁷b
[probably V¹³a]

etc.

The series VI⁷ resolving on Vb or V⁷ inverted is especially pleasant and worth noting:—

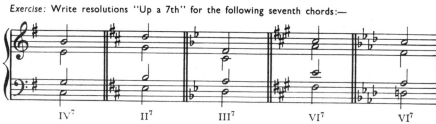

VI⁷Vb   VI⁷V⁷b   VI⁷bV⁷c   Ib   VI⁷cV⁷c   VIa   VI⁷dV⁷d   Ib

① The consecutive 9ths between bass and alto would probably have been vetoed by theorists until recently.

Exercise: Write resolutions "Up a 7th" for the following seventh chords:—

IV⁷   II⁷   III⁷   VI⁷   VI⁷

II⁷b   II⁷b   VI⁷c   (♯)VI⁷c   VII⁷

F.H. 2894

THE ADDED SIXTH CHORDS

[The following is a myth: an imaginary account of how these chords were discovered.]
Once upon a time a composer wrote a very ordinary Plagal Cadence:—

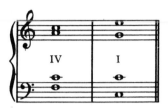

What happened after that we do not know; perhaps a performer misread the soprano part, perhaps a copyist made an error, but anyway the composer at the rehearsal heard:

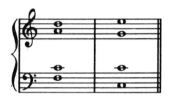

The Composer was not unduly startled, because the effect was not unpleasant and there were many other blunders to correct; but he made a note of what had occurred and later examined the spot. Then he took it around the corner to where a friend lived, a friend who was not a great composer but an excellent theorist. "Here, Joe", said the composer, "Look at this! It bothers me because it sounds very well and should sound bad. That first chord is II⁷b and should be followed by V. But I intended IV, and the D is an accident. Why does it sound well? Oddly enough, it does not even *sound* like II⁷; it still sounds like a queer kind of IV chord—I mean it sounds as if the root is F, not D. We went to the same harmony classes, but I don't remember old Bloggs showing us anything like that". "Nor do I", said Joe. "Leave it with me a day or two and I'll have a go at it". Well, three or four days later a haggard and white-faced Joe came around to the composer's house. "I've got it, Bill", he said, "but you had the secret all the time! Now then: that chord *is* a IV chord, but with a kind of *pimple* on it. After all, a nose can have a pretty big pimple on it and still be recognizable as a nose. So with the IV-chord: you can add a 6th to it and still go on with I if you treat it in a very special way. I call the pimple an Added Sixth, and these are the 'rules' I have worked out":—

Must be IV [Added Sixth] followed by I. ⎫
Or,   I   [Added Sixth] followed by V. ⎬ Both chords in *root* position.
—that is, the root moves "Up a 5th". ⎭

Both 5th and added 6th notes must be present—if you omit the 5th that is going too far and the chord will sound like IIb or VIb. But either of the notes can be higher than the other. The added 6th note moves up a step. The 5th stands firm.

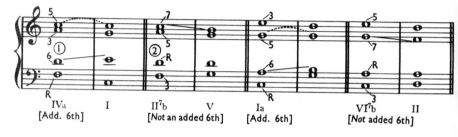

IVa	I	II⁷b	V	Ia		VI⁷b	II
[Add. 6th]		[*Not* an added 6th]		[Add. 6th]		[*Not* added 6th]	

Any chord which normally goes well before IV or I will go before them when 6th is added.

Just as with many words, so with some chords—the context determines the meaning. A dinner *table*, a multiplication *table*, a water *table* are all different uses of the same word, and we know which *meaning* to understand by the words surrounding that word.

So with chords: (1) sounds like a subdominant triad with a 6th added, whereas (2) sounds like a seventh-chord on D, first inversion: even though both chords are *spelt* identically.

IV [Added Sixth] and I [Added Sixth] may be used freely, to embellish any Plagal Cadence or Imperfect Cadence—introduce them freely. No special exercises are needed.

The other chords do not usually sound well with added sixths: but there seems to be no good reason why II [Added Sixth]—VI should be excluded from elementary textbooks: it is pleasant, unusual, and interesting:—

IV   II   VI
[Add. 6th]

TONALITY

—The mind's capacity for picking out the pitch of the Tonic very soon after a piece has commenced: like the needle of a compass, the mind searches for a few moments and then settles down "pointing" to the Keynote.

How is this faculty made to operate? Not by the first chord—this chord  might be

the first of a piece in C major, F, G, Bb, or E minor or E major—and some other keys also. As close to the beginning as possible, the composer writes V—I, V—VI, VIIb—I or VIIb—VI in the key he has chosen. This "establishes" the key.

Key is *changed* by the *same* method—by getting V—I or V—VI etc. of the NEW key. So the simplest method—called TRANSITION—has three chords like this:—

Some chord, often I, of the OLD key	V⁷ chord of the NEW key	Tonic chord, [or VI] of the NEW key

To make a smooth connection between first and second chords, find any notes *common* to them, and any notes *inflected* from first to second chords and GET THEM IN THE SAME VOICE in both chords:—

Example: G to F.   C to D.

Exercises: Write Transitions: (1) Eb to F, (2) F to D min., (3) D min. to Bb, (4) Bb to Gb, (5) Gb to Eb. —use signature of the FIRST key; remember ALL the accidentals proper to the NEW key.

Transition is most effective in the *middle* of a phrase, not usually *final* enough for use at the *end of* a phrase. To end a phrase, a more conclusive method is necessary, called **MODULATION**, which has four chords like this:—

Some chord, often I, of the OLD key	? Pivot	V⁷ chord of the NEW key	Tonic triad [or VI] of the NEW key

The pivot chord—in all elementary work, and most advanced work, pivot is always some form of II, IV, VI or [last choice] I♭ of the NEW key.

Therefore, scribble down <u>all</u> of these chords as triads, select the one closest to the Tonic triad of the Old key—i.e., the one which makes the best progression from the first chord. [Be *very* careful of accidentals, not to omit them.]

For example, C to D:—

—Obviously,  is the best one to follow Tonic triad of the Old key, so work it in smoothly—

G to D

G I

D IV   V⁷c   I

Notes: (1) Sometimes it happens that Tonic triad of the OLD key is itself II, IV, VI of the new key: then it will serve as its own pivot, and modulation can be completed in *three* chords, if desired:—

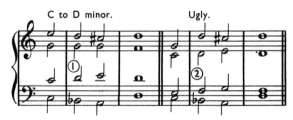

(2) If 7th note of V⁷ of the NEW key happens to be a factor of the pivot, it may be omitted—a plain V triad will do:—

Example: C to D—compare with first example above.

[—This is because a note lingers in one's mind until it is effectively contradicted, and we still hear the ghost of the G in our minds, through the A C♯ E triad.]

(3) 3rd or 5th of Pivot may be inflected—for various reasons, but usually to agree with the NEW key. DO NOT INFLECT THE ROOT—find some alternative chord instead:—

C to D minor.   Ugly.

—in chord ① 3rd was flattened to make the chord the true IVb of D minor—this sounds well. In chord ② the root was flattened to make a true VI triad of D minor—this makes an ugly wrench from 1st chord.

(4) It is sometimes awkward to reach a required major key directly:—

E♭ to G major.

The example is legitimate but Alto part E♭-E♮-D sounds false. But it is easy to reach the Tonic Minor of the required major key:—

In a case like this, it is perfectly legitimate* to modulate to the Tonic Minor and end with a Tièrce de Picardie:—

For reasons of chromatic harmony, to be explained later.

E♭   I   V1
Gmin.   IV   V   I(♮3)

(5) A properly-used Cadential 6 of the new key—
                              4

[Ic of the new key, on strong beat only, followed by V or V⁷ in root position.]

may be placed between Pivot and V of the new key. This will extend a 4-chord modulation to 5 chords, or a 3-chord modulation to 4 chords.

C to D.   C to G

This technique is also useful in dealing with such phrases as:

(y) (x)

—which obviously ends with a modulation to D. A pivot chord *could* be found to fit at (x) but it would be very awkward to manage—far better to make (x) Cadential Ic of the new key and have (y) as the Pivot:—

G
D

I   III
     VI   Ic   V⁷   I

What are these phrases where Ic between pivot and V⁷ helps?

When the note immediately before V⁷ of the [new] key is Tonic, Mediant, or Dominant of the new key—USE Ic for it: then Pivot is ONE CHORD TO THE LEFT.

Exercises:

    (1) Write 4-chord modulations [or 3-chord ones where possible]—
        (a) G to B minor; (b) G to B major; (c) B to F♯; (d) F♯ to E; (e) E to G; (f) D minor to E; (g) E to C♯ minor; (h) C♯ minor to A; (i) A to C; (j) C to E; (k) E to C. [Use signature of the *first* key in each case; remember *all* the accidentals!]

2) Write 3- or 4-chord modulations from (a) F to G minor; (b) F to Bb; (c) D to E minor; (d) A to E minor.

> (the above require the points in Note (3) above.)

3) from (a) F to A; (b) Eb to D; (c) Eb to C; (d) C to A; (e) A to C#.

> (the above require attention to Note (4) above.)

(4) (a) from E to B in 4 chords; (b) E to F# in 5 chords; (c) E minor to G in 4 chords; (d) G to E minor in 5 chords; (e) E minor to C in 5 chords.

> (See Note 5 above.)

(5) Add S.A.T.:—

(6) Add A.T.B.:—

Note (6)

A phrase may go through several keys on the way from key X to Y: these *middle* changes of key may be modulations, but they may also, very effectively, be transitions. The *final* change of key must be a *modulation*:—

Trans. to Eb   IIb
Mod. to G min.   Ic V I (T. de P.)
        Trans. to C min.
          Mod. C min. to D min.

64

(7) If a phrase moves, as it may, to a new key *early* in its course, then *remaining* in that key to the end of the phrase:—

—it is generally recommended that the *early* modulation should be V—Ib or V—VI, especially if the Tonic chord of new key happens to come on *strong* beat.

G   Ib   VIIb   Ia
D   IV   V⁷d Ib   II   V   Ia

or

G   Ib VIIb Ia
D   IV VIIb Ib   II⁷b Ic   V⁷   Ia

Exercises:
(1) Add A.T.B.:—

(a) (F major)

(b) (D minor)

(c)

(d)

F.H. 2894

(2) Add A.T.B.:

66

A favourite examination question reads something like this:—
   "Modulate from X to Y using this rhythm [which follows] in the Soprano part".

The object of this is to require of the candidate not a mere formula of chords but *a musical phrase.*

Method: First, write a 4-chord modulation—just the bare formula.
           Then re-copy it, embellishing it as follows:—

   Bass: No change, except time-values possibly.

   Harmony: Cadential Ic may be added as explained above, if it will help. Otherwise,
              NO CHANGE—the addition of a chord may ruin the whole thing.

   Soprano: Add passing notes, auxiliary-notes, or harmony-notes <u>within the same chords</u>
              to accommodate this to the given rhythm.

   Alto and Tenor: Some changes may be necessary to avoid "consecutives" etc. with the
                      re-arranged Soprano. Otherwise—no changes.

Example: G minor to E♭, using

in the Soprano.

Formula:— Expansion:—

—or, bar 3,
introducing Cad. Ic

Exercises: Modulate (a) from D to E; (b) E to C♯ minor; (c) D to F; (d) F to A—in each case
              using the above rhythm in the Soprano. Show both the formula and the expansion to
              your Teacher.

SUSPENSIONS

Compare these diagrams:—

The two passages are, of course, identical in harmony: the second has all the notes in the first with just four new ones to embellish it, and these are encircled. All are *discords*. These four notes are called suspensions: observe that they occur on the *strong* beats only.

Suspensions should be *prepared*—but (1) the 7th note of a seventh-chord will serve as preparation in place of a concord. Note-of-preparation may be tied to suspension or not, as desired.
In resolving, the suspended note falls a step—but all the other parts STAND FIRM AND WAIT FOR IT. Then all the parts can move forward together again. (2) There is only one exception— Leading-Note suspended may *rise* to resolve.—N.B.—*May*, not must—it often falls.

The above is the ordinary procedure. There is just one "Rule":—No voice, except bass sometimes, should strike the note-of-resolution *against* the suspended-note:—For example, suspended note F resolving on E, with E struck against the F:—

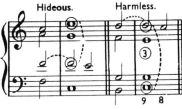

More advanced procedure:—
The chord-of-resolution may shift to a different *position* while suspended note is resolving:—

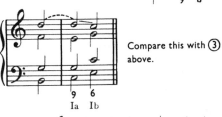

Compare this with ③ above.

Or, the chord-of-resolution may shift to a *new* chord while suspended note is resolving:—
[The new chord must make a good progression, and obviously must contain the note-of-resolution.]

Ornamental Resolution: exactly as given and illustrated in 5th Species Counterpoint:

Double and Triple Suspensions are very common—not at all infrequent. A double suspension was illustrated at ① and ② above. Triple suspension:

After 1600. A.D. Appoggiaturas are found: these are simply suspensions *without preparation*, but resolving just like any suspension. They were too harsh for 16th century ears but became common as soon as instrumental music arose. An accented passing-note is one form of appoggiatura. The following triple appoggiatura is quite common, especially at cadences:—

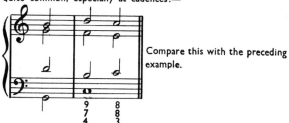

Compare this with the preceding example.

Figured Bass: Suspensions produce some quaint figuring! But it is logical if you remember always to count up the given interval *from the bass*, then recognize the note thus obtained for whatever it is. Experience cannot come except by practice.

Learn this *idiom*, which is not quite logical:—

[See also ④ in first example.]

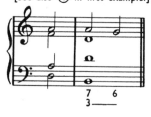

Also with 5 moving to 6, whether 5 is concord or not:—

Exercises:
(1) Decorate the following with suspensions:—

(2) Add S.A.T.:—

(3) Add S.A.T.   N.B.—Suspensions may occur even on _weak_ beats if they resolve _between_ the beats.

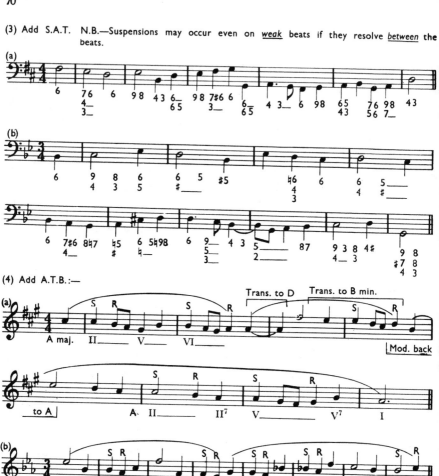

(4) Add A.T.B.:—

DOMINANT NINTH CHORD—V⁹

To the Dominant seventh chord add a ninth. In major key this can
be major or minor 9th.

—In minor key, use minor 9th only:—

Arrangement for S.A.T.B.:— Use root position *only* at present—i.e., root in bass.
9th must be present—or it would not be a 9th chord.
7th must be present.
Therefore from the chord of five notes, 3rd or 5th must be omitted.
9th, if major, must be *above* 3rd.

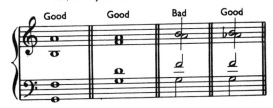

Definition: Any discord *wider* than 8ve [9th, 11th, 13th] is called a <u>Compound Discord</u>.
Any compound discord *may* resolve like a suspension or appoggiatura—that is:—with
the discord-note moving <u>a step</u> [generally downwards] while the other voices stand
firm and wait for it.

If 3rd is present in the 9th chord, 9th note may resolve like a
suspension, on the root:—

If 3rd is *not* present, 9th *must* resolve on 3rd before the harmony can change:—

Even these are pleasant
and unexpectedly easy to
sing:—

① is the only exception to ★ above: major 9th must be used here, because minor 9th used moving
to 3rd would produce an augmented 2nd interval.

72

Definition: "REAL Discord": when the chord moves to a *new* chord while the discord-note is resolving.

Real V^9 resolves on I or VI^7. 9th and 7th notes fall a step.

3rd rises a step.

Examples:

A compound discord will always eliminate the bad effect of a false relation: hence that between ① and ② is quite harmless, V^9 being a compound discord.

② must be *raised* Submediant to avoid augmented 2nd interval in the bass.

INVERSIONS of V^n—OMIT ROOT always: if 9th is present, root must be in the *bass* or else must be omitted:

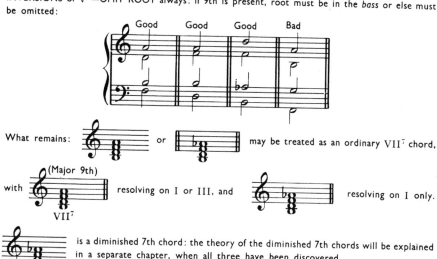

What remains: [music] or [music] may be treated as an ordinary VII^7 chord,

with [music] VII^7 resolving on I or III, and [music] resolving on I only.

[music] is a diminished 7th chord: the theory of the diminished 7th chords will be explained in a separate chapter, when all three have been discovered.

Exercises: (1) Write various arrangements for S.A.T.B. of V^9 in B minor, E♭ major, A♭ major, F♯ minor—all these in root position.

(2) Resolve the following in the style of suspensions or appoggiaturas:—

F.H. 2894

(3) Resolve the following as *real* V^9 chords, on I of each key:—

(4) Resolve the following as *real* V^9 chords, on VI^7 of each key:—

(5) Add S.A.T.:—[Symbolize all chords.]

(6) Add A.T.B.:—

IV V^9 V^7 I   II__ V^9 V^7 I   I   IV V^9 $\sharp$VI^7 V^{7}b V^{7}a VI   IIb V^9 I

DOMINANT ELEVENTH CHORD—V^{11}

This is *never* a "Real" discord—11th note always sounds like a 4th and resolves like a suspension or appoggiatura:—

3rd is omitted, and 11th note moves to 3rd:—

But 9th may be present and resolve on 3rd: then 11th moves up to 5th.

Exercises: (1) Add S.A.T.:—[Symbolize all chords.]

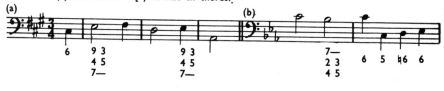

(2) Put a chord before and after each of these:—

DOMINANT THIRTEENTH CHORD—V^{13}

The whole series

Omit 5th if 13th is present.
Omit 3rd if 11th is present.

If 7th is present [it need not be] 13th should be above 7th.

In major key, 13th can be major or minor   } Similar to rules for
In minor key, use minor 13th only   } major and minor 9th.

Out of so many notes, and having 4 voices only, many different selections may be made by the composer—this makes V^{13} difficult to recognize sometimes. All the following selections are legitimate:—

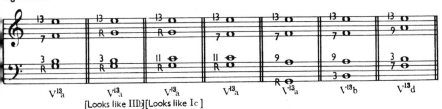

[Any of the 13th notes could be flattened.]

13th note may resolve in style of suspension or appoggiatura. 9th or 11th present will resolve along with 13th:—

REAL V^{13} resolves I or VI. 13th note may go to any note of Tonic triad. Normally it falls a third. [7th, 9th 11th behave as usual.]

Or, 13th note may stand firm:—

[Doubled major 3rd tolerable if root doubled also.]

F.H. 2894

:casionally, 13th note is found *rising* a third:—

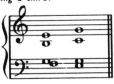

inor 13th if used in <u>*major*</u> key
ay also <u>*rise a semitone*</u>:

This last is often found written in "False Notation"—if you find a chord that looks like V⁷ with a sharpened 5th, that note is really a *minor 13th intended to rise:*

[D♯ = E♭ which is minor 13th *rising* to resolve.]

Exercises: (1) Write "Real" resolutions of the following V¹³ chords:—

(2) Add S.A.T.:—[Symbolize all chords.]

(3) Add A.T.B., using V^{13} where suggested:

CHROMATIC CHORDS

"Chromatic" in the ordinary colloquial sense simply means "containing accidentals" or "proceeding by semitones".

"Chromatic" has another more technical meaning—"Containing accidentals *which yet do* not *produce any modulation.* Compare these two diagrams:—

(1) is a diatonic chord—used to produce modulation to key G.

(2) is chromatic—the whole passage is in C—there is no modulation.

SUPERTONIC CHROMATIC CHORDS—II with ♯3.

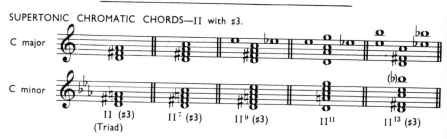

Supertonic chromatic chords normally resolve on a V *discord*—then ♯3 of II will fall a chromatic semitone to 7th of V chord

—or on I chord inverted—I*b* or I*c* [which will be a Cadential $\frac{6}{4}$ and must arrive on STRONG beat] and then ♯3 of II will *rise* a diatonic semitone.

II (♯3)—*Supertonic Chromatic Triad.*

—resolving on V⁷

—resolving on I inverted

F.H. 2894

II^7 (♯3)—*Supertonic Chromatic Seventh.*

—resolving on V^7
Then ♯3 of II falls a chromatic semitone.
    7th of II falls a step.

       I V^7c

—resolving on I inverted.
Then ♯3 of II rises a diatonic
    semitone.
    7th of II stands firm.

    Ib   Ib   etc.
                 Ic

The following exceptional treatment is always allowed, despite
the False Relation.

II (♯3) }
or II^7(♯3) } in first inversion only, going to V^7 in root position

  II_b(♯3) V^7a II^7_b(♯3) V^7a

Definition: "Fundamental Seventh Chord"—any seventh chord which has same quality of intervals
as V^7 chord, [i.e., major 3rd, perfect 5th, minor 7th] except V^7 itself.
Rule: Any Fundamental Seventh Chord *may* resolve with its 7th RISING, if 5th is present and
rises a similar interval.

This gives some new possibilities:—

If 5th rises a
step, 7th may
rise a step.
etc. If 5th rises a
third, 7th may
rise a third.

      V^7 Ic

Exercises: (1) Write (a) VI—II(♯3)—V^7—I in E♭, G, B, D.
             (b) I—II(♯3)—V^7—VI in E min., A min., C♯ min., F min.
             (c) Ib—IIb(♯3)—Cad. Ic—V—I in E, A♭, B♭, F.
             (d) IIb(♯3)—Ic—V^7—VI in G min., B♭ min., D min., F♯ min.
             (e) I—II(♯3)—Ib—II^7_b(♯3)—V^7a—I in G, E, D♭, B♭.

80

(2) Add S.A.T.:—[Symbolize all chords.]

(3) Add A.T.B., using the chords suggested:—

F.H 2894

Supertonic Chromatic Ninth Chords: $II^9(\sharp3)$

Same preliminaries as V^9—in major key, major or minor 9th are both good.
—in minor key, use minor 9th only.
—9th, if major, should be above 3rd.
Same resolutions in style of suspension or appoggiatura: [compare with V^9 diagrams].

REAL $II^9(\sharp3)$

—resolving on V^7.
9th, 7th fall a step.
$\sharp3$ falls a chromatic semitone.

—resolving on Ic [rarely Ib, or 3rd would be doubled in Ib].

9th and 7th stand firm.
$\sharp3$ rises a diatonic semitone—

Or, *minor* 9th used in *major* key may *rise* a chromatic semitone, going to Ic or V^{13}

INVERSIONS of $II^9(\sharp3)$—OMIT ROOT always, as in V^9.

What remains   or   may be treated just like root position, with

3rd, 7th, 9th behaving as usual:—

$II^9_d(\sharp3)$ V^7b $II^9_b(\sharp3)$ Ic

F.H. 2894

II *minor* 9th with its root omitted is a diminished 7th chord, and the general theory

of diminished sevenths will be given later.

Two points are worth mentioning here:—
II minor 9th dim. 7th may resolve on V minor 9th dim. 7th:

II minor 9th dim. 7th may resolve with the 9th *rising* a semitone in a major key:

But these are often written in False Notation, with sharpened root in place of minor 9th:—

D♯ = E♭ which is minor 9th intended to *rise*.

Compare with ① above, and notice that false notation will never be used when root is present in the *bass*.

Supertonic Eleventh Chord:—

—the 11th note is not chromatic, but if the 11th resolve upon ♯3rd of II, the result will be II⁷(♯3) or II¹¹(♯3).
—Same principles as V¹¹ —11th (or 4th) goes to 3rd.

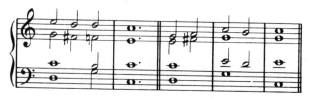

F.H. 2894

Supertonic Thirteenth Chord:—

—Same preliminaries as V^{13}

—Resolutions in style of suspension
or appoggiatura, similar to V^{13}:—

$II^{13}(\sharp 3)\,II^{7}(\sharp 3)\,V^{7}c \qquad I \qquad\qquad II^{9}\quad V^{9}{}_{b} \qquad I$
(VII^{7})

—"Real" Resolutions—similar to V^{13}, which see:—

Exercises:
(1) Resolve the following in the style of suspensions or appoggiaturas:—

(2) Write "real" resolutions of the following:—

84

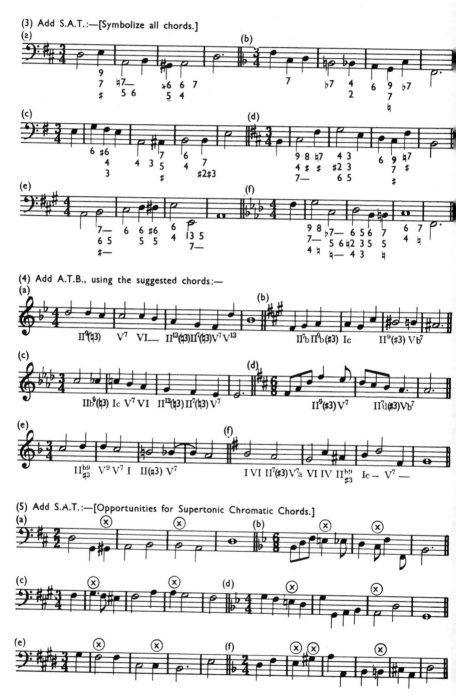

85

(6) Add A.T.B.:—

F.H. 2894

TONIC CHROMATIC CHORDS—I with ♭7

C major

C minor

N.B.—In minor key, 3rd is sharpened a semitone.

—These, if used chromatically, resolve in two different ways

—[A]—Upon Supertonic Chromatic concords or discords.
—then 7th, 9th, 11th and 13th will behave as usual.

Or—[B]—Upon Dominant *discords*: then ♭7th will rise a chromatic semitone and 9th, 11th and 13th will behave as usual.

In addition, any of the compound intervals may resolve like suspensions or appoggiaturas; but not the flattened 7th, so that the result will still be a tonic chromatic chord:—

Coming to the Real resolutions—[A]: ♭7th, 9th, fall a step. 13th most often falls a 3rd:—

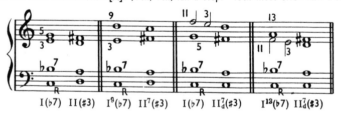

[B]—Upon V *discord* [i.e., not the triad] with ♭7 of I rising a chromatic semitone, 9th and 13th moving smoothly.

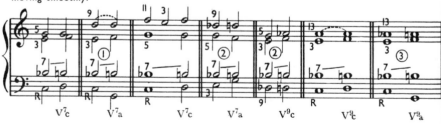

—Some of these, in diagram form, seem far-fetched and "hard to take"—but, skilfully used in the appropriate context by an ingenious composer, they are convincing and effective.

$VIIb$ will deputise for V^7. Observe the 9th standing firm at ① and minor 9th rising a semitone at ②; also notice the minor 13th rising at ③. This last is often written in false notation as—

Of course, in many cases the chord is used *not* chromatically:—

In this case the chord produces a modulation to F, at least in theory—though the modulation is very short and immediately contradicted by modulation back to C.

Or the chord may be approached as a diatonic chord in one key, and quitted as chromatic in another:—

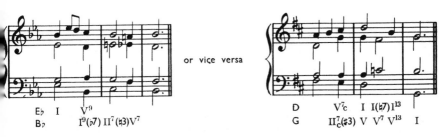

or vice versa

Eb I V^9
Bb $I^9(b7)\ II^7(\natural 3)V^7$

D V^7c I $I(\natural 7)I^{13}$
G $II^7_c(\natural 3)$ V $V^7\ V^{13}$ I

Exercises:
(1) Add S.A.T.:—

(2) Write (a) $Va-Ia(b7)-II^7_d(\sharp 3)-V^7_b-I$ in A, Eb.
    (b) $VI-IV$[Added 6th]$-Ia(b7)-II^0_d(\natural 3)-V^7_b-I$ in F minor, B minor.
            $(\natural 3)$
    (c) $I-VIIb-Ib-IV-Ib-I(\natural 7)-V^7_c-V^7_a-I$ in G, D.

88

(3) Add S.A.T.:—Treat these as *unfigured* basses except for the chords marked.

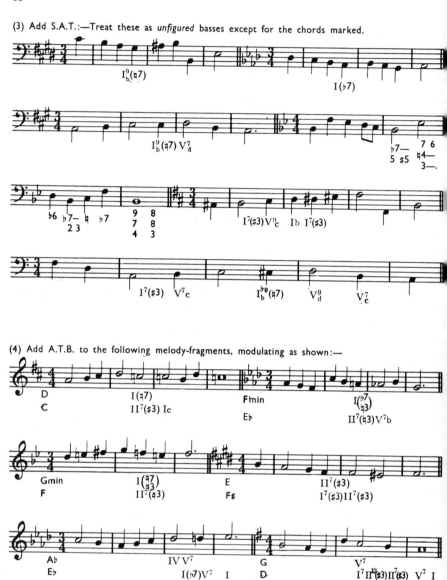

(4) Add A.T.B. to the following melody-fragments, modulating as shown:—

DIMINISHED-SEVENTH CHORDS

There are only three of these:

Definition: "Enharmonic change"—The difference between, for example, A♭ and G♯, or between
B♮ and C♭. There IS a difference between these pairs of notes but it is very slight and
is lost entirely in the process of tuning keyboard instruments to Equal Temperament—
ask your teacher about this. To all intents, therefore, "Enharmonic change" means a
change of name with *no* change of pitch.

By allowing enharmonic changes, EACH of the three diminished-seventh chords will
occur and can be used in EVERY major and minor key. Each will be found as either
Tonic minor 9th, or Supertonic minor 9th, or Dominant minor 9th, with the root
omitted in each case—as is normal in ninth-chords unless the root is in the bass.

Each diminished-seventh chord has four "True Roots"—find these by thinking *one
semitone below* each note in turn of the dim.-seventh chord.

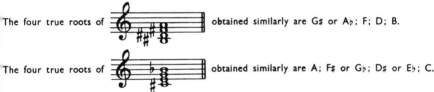

Thus, the four "True Roots" of ⟨chord⟩ are a semitone below A♭, namely G;

a semitone below F, which is E; a semitone below D, called C♯ or D♭; and a semitone
below B, viz., B♭ or A♯.

The four true roots of ⟨chord⟩ obtained similarly are G♯ or A♭; F; D; B.

The four true roots of ⟨chord⟩ obtained similarly are A; F♯ or G♭; D♯ or E♭; C.

Next, put a minor-ninth chord on each True Root in turn. Remember that a minor-ninth chord
consists of a major 3rd, perfect 5th, minor 7th, minor 9th; and adjust the notation by enharmonic
changes to achieve this.

A minor-ninth chord on G is

A minor-ninth chord on E is

A minor-ninth chord on C♯ is

A minor-ninth chord on B♭ is

Now take away the True Root in each case. What remains is a dim.-seventh chord—the SAME dim.-seventh chord in each case, but expressed with different notation:—

Derived from True Root

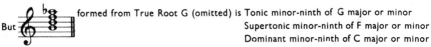

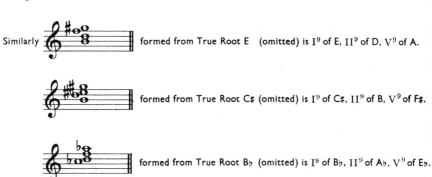

But ... formed from True Root G (omitted) is Tonic minor-ninth of G major or minor
Supertonic minor-ninth of F major or minor
Dominant minor-ninth of C major or minor

Similarly ... formed from True Root E (omitted) is I^9 of E, II^9 of D, V^9 of A.

... formed from True Root C♯ (omitted) is I^9 of C♯, II^9 of B, V^9 of F♯.

... formed from True Root B♭ (omitted) is I^9 of B♭, II^9 of A♭, V^9 of E♭.

To summarize:—

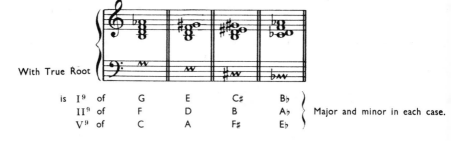

With True Root

is I^9 of   G   E   C♯   B♭
  II^9 of   F   D   B   A♭ } Major and minor in each case.
  V^9 of   C   A   F♯   E♭

Or, to sum it up in a different way, the combination B D F A♭, with proper enharmonic changes is V^9 in C, I^9 in C♯ or D♭, II^9 in D, V^9 in E♭, I^9 in E, II^9 in F, V^9 in F♯, I^9 in G, II^9 in A♭, V^9 in A, I^9 in B♭, II^9 in B—major or minor in each case.

Exercise: "Process" the other two dim.-seventh chords

—that is to say, find in each case the four true roots;
find the proper notation as a minor-ninth chord on each true root;
find the sense in which each would occur in every key.

RESOLUTIONS of Diminished-Seventh Chords.

Like any other compound discord, the 9th note from the True Root of a dim. seventh chord will resolve in the style of a suspension or appoggiatura, moving down one semitone (to the True Root) while the other notes stand firm. The result is a fundamental seventh-chord in each case:—

I($\flat$7)	of G	E	C$\sharp$	B$\flat$.
II^7($\sharp$3)	of F	D	B	A$\flat$.
V^7	of C	A	F$\sharp$	E$\flat$.

—which is then resolved accordingly.

Exercise: Arrange  for S.A.T.B. and resolve in all keys in style

of suspensions, as shown above.

REAL resolutions:—V^9 dim. 7th chords normally resolve on Tonic triads.

II^9 dim. 7th chords normally resolve on V^7 or V^9 chords.

I^9 dim. 7th chords normally resolve on II($\sharp$3) triads or discords, or on V discords.

—The behaviour of 3rd, 7th, 9th is as explained in the previous chapters.

Example: resolving the combination B,D,F,A$\flat$ in all keys: major key signatures used in each case.

First as V^9 resolving on I 9th and 7th fall a step, 3rd rises a step.

Notes: (1) V^9_c if resolved on Ia will produce consecutive fifths.

∴ *Resolve* V^9_c *on* I$\flat$; then 7th may rise, as in V^-_c–I$\flat$.

(2) V^9_e if resolved directly will produce an unpleasant Ic chord.

∴ *Resolve 9th in the bass as a suspension on the True Root, producing* V^-_h, which can then resolve in the usual way.

Secondly, as II^9, resolving
on V^7 or V^9
9th and 7th fall a step.
3rd falls a chromatic semitone.

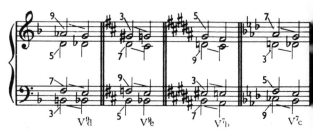

Lastly, as $Ib^9(b7)$, resolv-
ing on $II^7(\sharp3)$ or $II^9(\sharp3)$.
9th and 7th fall a step.
[Resolutions on V dis-
cords would also be poss-
ible.]

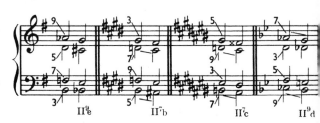

Exercises: Resolve 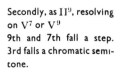 and [chord] arranged for S.A.T.B. in any convenient
way, as V^9 on I of each key, then as II^9 on V^7 or V^9, then as I^9 on $II(\sharp3)$ or on V^7 or V^9. Use
major key signatures for some, and minor signatures for others.

Any Dim. 7th chord may be used as a pivot chord in modulation by approaching it as I^9, II^9, or V^9
in one key and quitting it as I^9, II^9 or V^9 in another key—a most valuable means of modulation. A
few examples will be sufficient to make this quite clear. Using [chord] in various ways:—

| Approached as C major | V^9 | | | G maj. | I^9 | | | | F min. | II^9 | | |
| Quitted as Ab major | II^9 | V^7 | I | A min. | V^9 | Ib | | | Db maj. | $I^9(b7)$ | II^7 | V^7 | I |

Exercise: Using the key-signature of the *first* key, but writing the dim. 7th chord with notation proper to the *new* key,

Use to modulate from: (1) A to D; (2) D min. to B min.; (3) A♭ to D♭.

Use to modulate from: (4) A to D; (5) D min. to B min.; (6) A♭ to D♭.

Use to modulate from: (7) G to E; (8) B to G; (9) F♯ minor to B♭.

Further notes: As was explained earlier, II^9 dim. 7th may resolve on V^9 dim. 7th chord—this was a logical extension of II^9 resolving on V^7 and is used chiefly to avoid unpleasant consecutive 5ths:

The following is a *new* principle: owing to the highly ambiguous nature of the chord, ANY dim. 7th chord may be followed by ANY OTHER dim. 7th chord, ascending or descending, provided all voices move one semitone. Resolve the LAST dim. 7th chord in any of the various ways:—

ANY convenient notation may be employed—whatever is most readable.

There are very many examples of this in the works of 19th century composers, especially Liszt; the effect is too saccharine for many 20th century ears.

Debussy, Ravel, and the other French Impressionist composers extended the idea of parallel dim. 7th chords, with only the last one resolved, to other qualities of 7th chords, 9th chords and even 11th chords.

CHROMATIC TRIADS

[A.] Any triad belonging to a minor key (both forms) may be borrowed for use in its Tonic Major.

—all these triads belong to C minor in harmonic or melodic forms, but are here shown in notation proper to C major—as they would appear if borrowed into that key.   Very few "rules" can be given —the ♭III chords and the ♭VII chord had better be avoided entirely by beginners; the chords involving the flattened submediant:—

II(♭5)   IV(♭3)   ♭VI(♭5)   will be of most use.

Often the 7th (from minor scale) can be added with good effect to each triad
Example:

IV(♭3) II⁷(♭5)   ♭VI(♭5) IV(♭3)
[Added 6th]

Most often the chords are useful as chromatic in one key and diatonic in another in the process of modulation. For example, the IV(♭3) chords above would serve as excellent pivot chords from C major into E♭(II) or A♭(VI); or approached as diatonic in A♭ or F minor or D♭ and quitted as IV in C minor or IV (♭3) in C major. The following diagrams will make this clear.

C   I   IV(♭3)
E♭   II   V⁷   I   A♭   VI   V⁷b   I

A♭ I   VI   D♭ I   III
C   IV(♭3) V⁷————   I   C   IV(♭3) V⁷— —

This explains why, in the chapter on modulation, we were safe in saying that the 3rd or the 5th, but not the root, of a pivot chord could be inflected; and also that sometimes it is easier to get to the tonic minor of a required major key than directly to that major key; and that these methods were legitimate. In the four diagrams above, note that in the first two the 3rd of the pivot is inflected, as compared with the first key; and in the last two the modulation is made as if to C minor, ending with a Tierce de Picardie.

B.] More remote chromatic triads such as in C major

scarcely come within the scope of an elementary note-book. However, those above may be used (1) if the chord before and after contain at least one note in common like this:—

OR (2)—in $\frac{6}{3}$ position, with a diatonic $\frac{6}{3}$ before and the same diatonic $\frac{6}{3}$ afterwards; three of the four parts should move like auxiliary-notes:—

Bear in mind, we are speaking of strictly chromatic uses, in which such chords will appear as bold and refreshing splashes of colour. In the course of *modulation* such chords appear frequently and logically.
Because of the nature of this book, many other chromatic uses of triads [such as Bach's magnificent use of III(♯3) before IIb at a cadence] will have to be left to the serendipity of the student.

[C.] The NEAPOLITAN triad is very useful and beautiful. It is the major common chord on the flattened supertonic of a major or minor key:

and it has the unexpected property of leading to the V triad, or V discords, or Cadential Ic:—

This effect is called the " Pathetic Cadence " and is common in instrumental music.

For _vocal_ purposes the augmented 4th or dim. 5th leap in the bass is unsatisfactory.
Therefore:—Use Neapolitan triad in $\frac{6}{3}$ position [then it is called the Neapolitan Sixth, not to be confused with Italian, French, and German Sixths, which are augmented sixth chords.]
Double its 3rd—i.e., the bass note.
Disregard the false relations indicated—they are harmless.

The dim. 3rd leap in Soprano is also unexpectedly easy to sing, and quite harmless.

The approach: I-Neap. 6th is good, also IV, IV(♭3), ♭VI in major key—beware of false relations in the approach.
The chord is very often used in modulation, when the above Neap. 6th in C might be approached as I of D♭, IV of A♭, VI of F minor, ♭VI of F major, V of G♭ etc.:—

Exercises:—

(1) Write (a) I—IV(♭3)—V—♭VI—IV(♭3)—V—I in G, B♭, E♭.
      (b) I—IIb(♭5)—Ib—IV(♭3)—II⁷(♭5)—V—I in F, A, D.
      (c) I—IVb(♭3)—IIb(♭5)—V—Ib—IV(♭3)—IV(♭3) (Added 6th)—I in A♭, E.
      (d) V—I—IV(♭3)—Neap. Sixth—V—I in F, A, B.
      (e) I—♭VIb—Vb—I—IV(♭3)—V⁷—♭VI in D, A, E.
      (f) Ib—Neap. 6th—V⁷♭—I in B, F♯, E.

(2) Write modulations using  as pivot-chord, from (a) E to G; (b) G to E; (c) E to C.

   Write modulations using as pivot-chord, from (d) D to F; (e) E♭ to D; (f) D to A♭.

   Write modulations using as pivot-chord, from (g) C to F♯; (h) B to F♯.

(3) Write short passages, using (in root position or first inversion)

(a)   in D,   (b)   in B♭

(4) Add A.T.B.:—

(a) [A major]   (b) [B♭ major]

(c) [G major]   (d) [D♭ major]

(e) [A♭ major]   (f) [E major]

(g) [B♭ major]

AUGMENTED SIXTH CHORDS

Write the Supertonic Minor 9th chord  and then flatten its 5th:—

Then, Italian Augmented Sixth comprises ♯3rd, ♭5th, 7th of this chord.
French Augmented Sixth comprises root, ♯3rd, ♭5th, 7th of this chord.
German Augmented Sixth comprises ♯3rd, ♭5th, 7th, ♭9th of this chord.
In classical usage, the flattened 5th of the chord is always the bass note:—

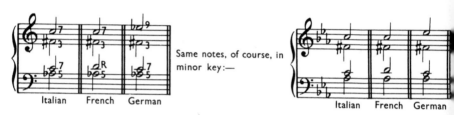

Same notes, of course, in minor key:—

—and the chord takes its name from the Augmented 6th interval which occurs between its 5th as bass note and the 3rd in some higher voice. No other chord in classical harmony has this interval. The chord, being really a doubly-chromatic II discord, normally resolves on V or Cadential Ic. The two notes which form the aug. 6th interval *repel* one another to form an 8ve on the dominant:—

N.B.—Consecutive Perfect 5ths *are allowed* in resolving German Sixth.

Any chord which will lead to II will lead to all these augmented sixth chords—but beware of augmented intervals in approaching ♭5 in the bass.

Another series of augmented sixth chords is formed of V_7 and V minor 9th with 5th flattened:—

—giving rise to:

Italian   French   German

—with 5th as bass-note. Any chord which will lead to V will lead to these. Since these are all chromatic V discords, they all resolve on I, or Appogg. IVc chord. The notes forming the aug. 6th interval repel one another as in the II series, to form an 8ve on the Tonic:—

Italian Ia   Italian IVc   Ia   French Ia   German IVc   Ia

As has been said, the flattened 5th of the chords is normally the bass-note. Very occasionally the 3rd is found in the bass, the chord being a German Sixth "inverted", $\frac{7}{5}$ from bass. This will be identifiable by the dim. 3rd interval not found elsewhere in classical usage, and these notes *attract* one another to form an 8ve:—

Instead of the above "Real" resolutions, various others, with one or more voices moving like suspensions or appoggiaturas, may be found and may be used:—

The enharmonic possibilities will be discussed later.

Exercises:

(1) Write IVb—Italian 6th of II—Va —Ia in F, G minor.

VIa—French 6th of II—Ic—Va —Ia in A, Eb.

VIa—II⁷c—German 6th of II—Va —Ia in C, E minor.

IIa—Italian 6th of V—I in E, Bb.

II⁷a—French 6th of V—IVc—I in D, Bb minor.

V⁷c—German 6th of V—I in F♯, D minor.

(2) Complete the following fragments, adding S.A.T.:—

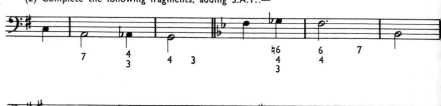

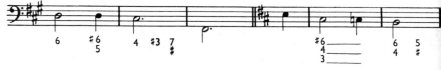

F.H. 2894

Enharmonic equivalents:—

The German Sixth in C:—  is the same as which is $\begin{cases} V^7 \text{ of } D\flat. \\ II^7(\natural 3) \text{ of } G\flat. \\ I(\flat 7) \text{ of } A\flat. \end{cases}$

It may be approached as an Augmented Sixth and quitted as a Fundamental Seventh in one of those keys, or, vice versa, approached in D♭ or G♭ or A♭ and quitted as German Sixth in C:—

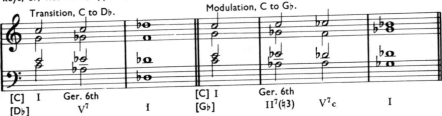

Transition, C to D♭.   Modulation, C to G♭.

[C]	I	Ger. 6th		[C]	I	Ger. 6th		
[D♭]		V⁷	I	[G♭]		II⁷(♮3)	V⁷c	I

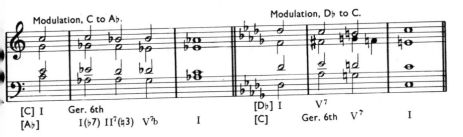

Modulation, C to A♭.   Modulation, D♭ to C.

[C]	I	Ger. 6th			[D♭]	I	V⁷	
[A♭]		I(♭7) II⁷(♮3) V⁷♭	I		[C]		Ger. 6th V⁷	I

Similarly, with the German Sixth of V:—

[C]	I Ger. 6th		[C]	I	Ger. 6th		[C]	I	Ger. 6th	
[G♭]	V⁷	I	[B]		II⁷(♯3) V⁷c	I	[D♭]		I(♭7) II⁹(♮3) V⁷♭	I

—Some of the above, though *possible*, are rather far-fetched: to be used only *very* rarely and for special effects. Others are quite convincing. Write the chord in question with notation proper to the NEW key in each case.

Exercises: Use (1) 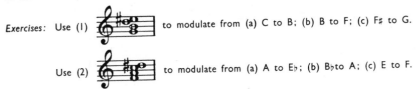 to modulate from (a) C to B; (b) B to F; (c) F♯ to G.

Use (2) to modulate from (a) A to E♭; (b) B♭ to A; (c) E to F.

PEDAL POINTS, PEDAL NOTES, OR MERELY PEDALS

—These are held (or repeated) notes, normally in the bass. Any degree of the scale may be held as a pedal, but much the commonest are Tonic [producing a feeling usually of finality, or security, or affirmation] or the Dominant [insecurity, struggle, questioning]—and sometimes both together. The name is taken from the organ, of course, which can hold a pedal note indefinitely—and very often does, while the organist extemporizes indefinitely above it—but pedal notes occur also on bagpipes: any piece called "Musette", which is the French name for bagpipes [like the one in D in the Anna Magdalena Notebook of J. S. Bach] will be found to be largely written above a pedal-point. Pieces of a pastoral character, like the pastoral symphony in the "Messiah", are commonly written over pedal points. Many other well-known examples include the opening of the St. Matthew Passion, the opening of Brahms' Symphony No. I, the Bourrée in the English Suite in A minor of J. S. Bach, and the end of the J. S. Bach organ Passacaglia—Tonic and Mediant pedal notes, in the upper parts, decorated with auxiliary-notes.

Rules: The *first* chord with the Pedal, and the *last*, should be in harmony with it. In between, anything may happen, even modulation.

The lowest *moving* part (Tenor usually) must make a good bass (avoiding bad 6 chords)
4
except where pedal-note happens to be a factor of the chord:

In elementary work, students will need pedal-note technique probably in only one problem:—

Given: A long held Tonic or Dominant at the *end* of an unfigured bass.

Method: Take the *first* few notes of the Soprano part, and *repeat* them, as many as convenient, reharmonized over the pedal at the end:—

Suppose the working began:

Then a three-bar Tonic pedal ending might be arranged as:—

GROUND BASS

—A composition in which a theme is repeated several times consecutively, normally in the bass, with variations above it.

—This is a more-or-less instrumental form: in working it the range-limitations of *human* voices may be exceeded.

Classical examples: J. S. Bach—Passacaglia for organ.

—The Chaconne in D minor for violin unaccompanied is really a ground bass.

Purcell —Introduction to the anthem "Rejoice in the Lord alway".

Evening hymn on a ground.

Dido's Lament, from "Dido and Aenaes".

—and many others. Purcell used this form frequently.

Brahms —Finale of the Variations on a theme of Haydn.

Finale of 4th Symphony is really a ground bass.

—Be sure to study some of the above before attempting questions like the following.

A favourite form of question is: "Make three presentations of the following ground bass. Show some two-part writing, some three-part, some four-part, and include some chromatic chords in the last presentation".

—This is largely a *rhythmic* problem: it *might* be possible to find three different ways of harmonizing *some* ground-bass themes, but not very many.   An infinite number of rhythmic figures could be found, however.

Method: Copy given ground bass 4 times—one more than the number asked for, because it is taken for granted that

(1) is bass unaccompanied.

(2) —add Tenor. Invent a two-bar rhythmic figure [something *very* simple] and develop it by repeating the rhythm at different pitches so that bar 6=4=2 and bar 5=3=1 *in rhythm*—see example below. Keep (2) diatonic in home key.

(3) Add Alto. Get a *new* two-bar rhythmic figure [still simple, though not quite so simple as before] and develop it as before.

Modulate to one or two closely-related keys—a modulation to the Dominant at the *end* of the variation is particularly appropriate.

(4) Add Soprano. Introduce a *new* two-bar rhythmic figure in the Soprano—a little less simple than the others, but not too complicated.

Modulate and/or make transitions *freely*—then some of the chords used will almost certainly be chromatic in one key or the other.

Get a *climax* somewhere near the end—an accented high note in Soprano will do.

Example: The following is *not* a specially "worked-up" example of perfection, but the first that came into our head:—

The final tonic triad is added to the ground-bass after the *last* variation only, to make an ending. Sometimes a short coda, on a tonic pedal, is asked for: then one good way of working is to take the ground-bass theme [or a version of it] into the Soprano part, combining it with the last rhythmic figure, the whole over the tonic pedal, thus:—

Exercises: Treat the following as shown above:—